THE BIBLE
for Children

Presented to

....

on the occasion of

....

with love from

....

Val Biro (1921–2014) was born in Budapest, Hungary as Balint Stephen Biro, and moved to England in 1939 when he came to study at the Central School of Arts in London. Through a long career spanning over 70 years, his illustrations appeared in over 400 books worldwide, and on the covers of many more. He was a renowned and much-loved author and illustrator of children's books.

ISBN 978-1-78270-291-7

This edition first published 2017

Published by Award Publications Limited,
The Old Riding School, Welbeck,
Worksop, S80 3LR

www.awardpublications.co.uk

17 1

Printed in China

THE BIBLE
for Children

Illustrated by Val Biro

AWARD PUBLICATIONS LIMITED

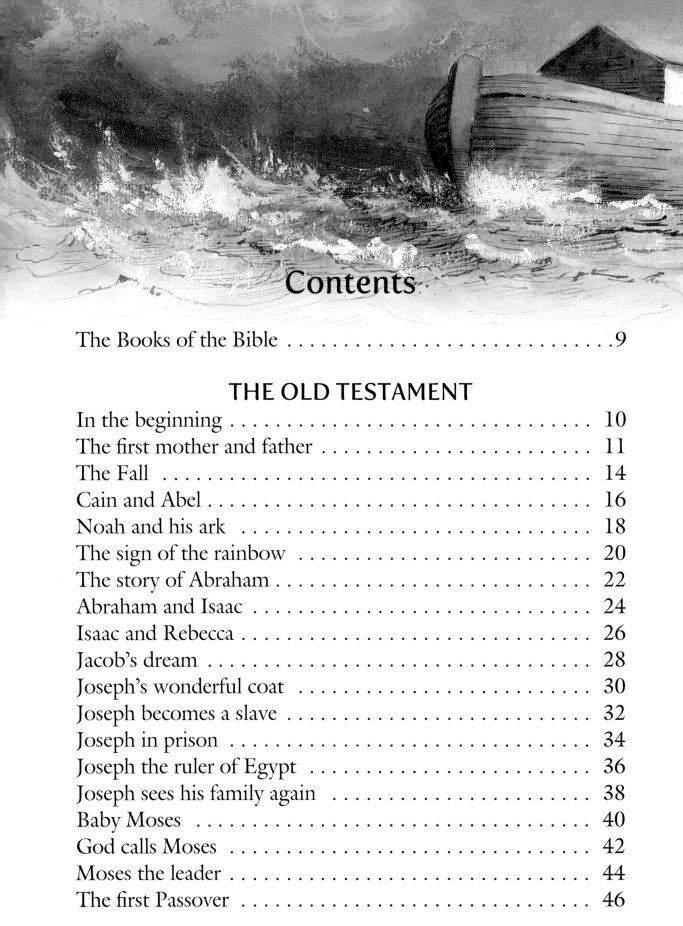

Contents

THE NEW TESTAMENT

MAPS

The books of the Bible

THE OLD TESTAMENT

Genesis	2 Chronicles	Daniel
Exodus	Ezra	Hosea
Leviticus	Nehemiah	Joel
Numbers	Esther	Amos
Deuteronomy	Job	Obadiah
Joshua	Psalms	Jonah
Judges	Proverbs	Micah
Ruth	Ecclesiastes	Nahum
1 Samuel	Song of Songs	Habakkuk
2 Samuel	Isaiah	Zephaniah
1 Kings	Jeremiah	Haggai
2 Kings	Lamentations	Zechariah
1 Chronicles	Ezekiel	Malachi

THE NEW TESTAMENT

Matthew	Ephesians	Hebrews
Mark	Philippians	James
Luke	Colossians	1 Peter
John	1 Thessalonians	2 Peter
Acts	2 Thessalonians	1 John
Romans	1 Timothy	2 John
1 Corinthians	2 Timothy	3 John
2 Corinthians	Titus	Jude
Galatians	Philemon	Revelation

THE OLD TESTAMENT

In the beginning

Genesis 1:1–2:3

Many years ago, there was just God. He made everything. At first there was just water and empty darkness.

Then God made light. He divided light from dark and called the light "day" and the darkness "night".

Then God made the sky and the mighty heavens. God looked at all he had made and was pleased with it.

Then God made dry land rise up out of the water. God called the land "earth" and the water "sea". He made plants and trees to cover the earth.

Next, God put lights in the sky: the sun to brighten the day and the moon and stars to light up the night.

Then God made all kinds of animals and birds to live on the earth and fill the skies, and fish to fill the seas.

God looked at all these things and was pleased with them. Then God made men and women to live on the earth. He made them just like himself, to be his friends. God blessed the people he had made and told them to have families and fill the earth, and to take care of all the plants and animals.

When God had finished making heaven and earth, he rested. He looked down from heaven on everything he had created, and saw that it was all very good indeed.

The first mother and father

Genesis 2:4–24

When God made the dry land rise up out of the water, nothing could live there at first. So God made streams to flow from the ground and water the land. The dry earth turned to mud, which God took and formed into the figure of a man. Then he breathed into the figure and gave it life. The name of this first living person was Adam.

God planted a beautiful garden for Adam, filled with trees and flowers. In the centre of this Garden of Eden grew the tree of the knowledge of good and evil. God told Adam that he could eat any of the fruits of the trees, except those growing on the tree of knowledge.

After a while, God saw that Adam needed a friend and helper. He shaped all the wild animals and birds from the soil, but none of these was a suitable companion for Adam. So God made Adam fall into a deep sleep, and took a rib bone from him. Then he made a woman out of the rib bone and brought her to Adam. Adam called her Eve, and loved her dearly. And Adam and Eve were the father and mother of all people on earth.

The Fall
Genesis 3:1–24

Of all the creatures that God made, the serpent was the most cunning. It crept up to Eve and asked her if it was true they weren't supposed to eat the fruit from any of the trees in this garden.

"We may eat the fruit of any of the trees," said Eve, "but not that of the tree in the middle of the garden. We may not touch it, or we will die."

The snake told her that it was not true. The fruit would give them wonderful knowledge. They would be like gods.

So Eve picked some of the fruit and ate it. Then she took some to Adam and gave it to him to eat. Immediately, their eyes opened and they realised that they were naked. So they sewed together some fig leaves to cover themselves.

Just then, they heard God walking in the garden. Adam and Eve hid among the trees because they were ashamed. God asked them both what they had done. Adam said, "The woman you made from me and for me, she gave me the fruit of the tree, and I ate it."

And Eve said, "The serpent, he told me to eat it!"

God was very angry. Because they had disobeyed him, God sent Adam and Eve out of the Garden of Eden forever. From then on, Adam would have to work and find his own food to live. Life would not be easy any longer.

And God told the snake, "You are the most cursed of all creatures. You and the woman will always be enemies, and one day her child will crush your head and you will strike his heel!"

DID YOU KNOW?
The first book of the Bible tells of a serpent tempting Eve. The last book of the Bible calls Satan, "that serpent of old, who is the Devil".
(Genesis 3; Revelation 20:2)

Cain and Abel

Genesis 4:1–16

Adam and Eve eventually had two sons. The oldest was Cain the other was Abel. Abel became a shepherd looking after flocks of sheep, while Cain worked on the land, growing crops for food.

After a time, Cain brought some of his produce as an offering to God. Abel brought an offering of the best lambs from his flocks. God was pleased with Abel and his offering, but he did not accept Cain or his gifts.

Cain was angry and disappointed. He became very jealous of Abel.

God warned Cain to be careful: "Sin is crouching at your door like a wild animal ready to pounce!" He meant the evil feelings lurking inside Cain's heart.

But Cain took no notice. Instead, Cain invited Abel to go for a walk in the countryside with him. As soon as they reached a lonely place, Cain attacked his brother and killed him.

"Where is your brother?" asked God, when Cain returned.

Cain pretended not to know. "I can't be expected to look after him!" he said.

"What have you done?" said God. "I can hear your brother's blood crying out to me from the ground. From now on, the ground will never give you any food. You will be a restless wanderer for the rest of your life."

Cain begged God not to give him such a harsh punishment. If he had to leave God's presence and wander the earth, his life would be in great danger. So God put a special mark on Cain to make sure that no one would harm him. Cain left and went to live in the land of Nod, east of Eden.

DID YOU KNOW?
The word 'sin' appears over 4,000 times in the Bible. It is first mentioned not, as one might expect, in the story of the Fall, but in the tale of Cain and Abel.

Noah and his ark

Genesis 6:5–7; 7:1–10

God had created Adam and Eve so that their descendants would fill the earth. He wanted them to be kind and loving to each other.

Instead, God saw that there was a great deal of wickedness in their hearts, and it made him very sad.

"I shall rid the earth of all its people, as well as all the animals, plants, creeping things and birds of the heavens, for I am sorry I created them."

But there was one man who pleased God, and that was Noah, who was always his loyal servant.

DID YOU KNOW?
The word 'ark' means a place of safety and refuge. The Ark of the Covenant was a special box in which the Ten Commandments given to Moses were kept safe.

God explained to Noah what he had decided to do: "I am going to cause a great flood to destroy all life. I want you to make an ark out of strong wood. Cover it with pitch to make it waterproof. Then take your family into the ark, along with two of every kind of animal. In this way, I will be able to start afresh."

Noah did just as God had told him. He made his ark strong and safe, and then he filled it with his entire family, and a pair of every kind of bird and animal. Then God shut the door and the storms came.

The sign of the rainbow
Genesis 7:11–9:17

The rain fell for forty days. First the waters covered the land and filled the valleys. Then they covered the hills. Finally they covered the mountains. Every living thing was drowned. But Noah and his family were safe in the ark with all the animals, just as God had planned.

Eventually it stopped raining, but it was still a long time before the waters started to go down. After two months, Noah sent out first a raven and then a dove to look for signs of dry land, but there was nothing. Then he sent out the dove again, and this time it came back with an olive leaf in its beak. Now Noah knew that the earth was becoming dry again.

DID YOU KNOW?

The ark was said to measure 300 cubits (137 metres) long, 50 cubits wide and 30 cubits high. This would mean that the ark was around half as long as the largest cruise ship today.

Noah left the ark on dry land and immediately he made an altar to worship God and give thanks for their safety.

God blessed Noah and his sons: "Fill the earth with children," he told them. "Look after the animals and birds, trees and plants. Follow my ways and I will always be your God."

Then he made a solemn promise to Noah. "Never again will a flood destroy all living creatures, or the earth be covered in water. There will be time to sow seed and harvest crops, cold and heat, summer and winter, day and night. I will put my rainbow in the heavens as a sign of my promise to you and your children and every living creature in the world."

The story of Abraham
Genesis 12:1–9

Abraham was a rich man who lived in the city of Ur, in Mesopotamia. He was devoted to God and had been obedient to him all his life. When Abraham was seventy-five years old, God called him and said: "Leave your home and go to the new land I shall show you. I will be your God and will bless you and your family."

Abraham trusted God. He took his wife, Sarah, his nephew, Lot, their servants, sheep and goats and everything they owned, and set off in search of the land of Canaan, stopping only whenever they found water for their animals.

DID YOU KNOW?
Before Isaac's birth, Sarah thought she would be unable to have children, so her handmaiden, Hagar, bore Abraham a son, named Ishmael.

Abraham continued travelling through Canaan until he reached the holy place of Shechem. There, God appeared to him again. "Look all around you. I am going to give this land to you and your descendants."

Abraham travelled on towards the mountains. Again, God appeared to him. "Look up at the stars," he said. "There are too many to count. I promise you that one day your descendants will be just as numerous!"

Now Abraham trusted God, but he was worried because he and Sarah had no children. His wife was now too old to have them. But nothing was impossible to God and in time, just as he had promised, Sarah gave birth to a little boy and they called him Isaac. Now Abraham could indeed be the father of many people.

Abraham and Isaac

Genesis 22:1–19

After a few years had passed, God tested Abraham to see if he was still faithful to him.

"Abraham!" he called. "Take your son Isaac, whom you love so much, and offer him as a sacrifice on the mountain I shall show you."

Early next day, Abraham saddled up his donkey. He chopped some wood to make a fire for the sacrifice and gave the bundle to Isaac to carry. Then, together with two servants, they set off on their journey.

On the third day Abraham knew they had reached the right place. He told the servants to stay at their camp. Then he and Isaac continued up the mountain, with Isaac carrying the wood and Abraham carrying the container of hot coals for the fire.

After a while, Isaac turned to Abraham and asked him: "Father, we have the fire and the wood for the sacrifice, but where is the lamb?"

DID YOU KNOW?

In the past, many religions have practiced sacrifices as a way to gain favour with their gods and show faithfulness.

"My son," said Abraham, "God himself will provide the lamb."

Abraham built an altar and arranged the wood around it. Then he tied Isaac's hands and feet and laid him on the altar, on top of the wood. He then took up his knife and stretched out his hand to kill his son.

But an angel from God stopped him. "Abraham!" he said. "Do not harm the boy. God knows that you are indeed faithful to him, and that you would do anything for him, even sacrifice your son." Abraham looked up and saw a ram stuck in the bushes nearby. He took it and offered it as a sacrifice to God in place of Isaac.

Together, he and Isaac went back down the mountain and returned home.

Isaac and Rebecca
Genesis 24:1–67

Abraham was very old, and Sarah had already died, by the time Isaac had grown up. Abraham knew that he must find a wife for Isaac so that his family could increase and become the people of God.

He sent his most faithful servant, with a string of camels laden with gifts, to Mesopotamia to find a wife for Isaac from among his people there.

It was evening when the servant arrived: the time of day when the women came outside the gates of the city in order to fetch water from the well. Abraham's servant prayed, asking God to give him a sign to help him choose the right wife for Isaac. He would ask for a drink at the well. The young woman who offered to water his camels would be the one chosen by God.

Even before he had finished praying, a beautiful young woman came up to the well to fill her water jug. The servant asked her if she could spare him a drink.

"Drink, my lord," she said, and she held out her jug for him. "And when you have finished, I'll draw some water for your camels as well." The servant knew he had found the wife for Isaac.

The young woman's name was Rebecca. Her father gave his blessing to the marriage, and Rebecca was willing to return at once with Abraham's servant.

Early next morning they set out for Canaan. Isaac was praying out in the fields when he saw the camel train coming. He ran to meet them and took Rebecca by the hand. He loved her immediately. They married and lived together in great happiness.

DID YOU KNOW?
It was common at this time for families to choose a spouse for their sons and daughters. Children could be betrothed, or promised to each other, as young as 12 years old.

Jacob's dream

Genesis 27:1–33:20

Isaac and Rebecca had two sons. Esau, the eldest, became a hunter. He had the birthright to his father's inheritance. Jacob, the younger son, became a sheep farmer and was his mother's favourite. When Isaac was old and dying, Jacob tricked Esau out of his birthright with the help of his mother, Rebecca. But afterwards, Esau was so furious with his brother that Jacob had to flee for his life. He headed for Mesopotamia.

On the way, he stopped for the night in a lonely, rocky place, where he slept on the ground. That night Jacob had a strange dream. He saw a ladder stretching right up to heaven, and God's angels were going up and down it. Then he saw God himself standing beside him, saying, "I am the God of your grandfather Abraham, and your father Isaac. I shall be with you and bless you, and keep you safe. The land on which you are lying will be yours, and from you will come my chosen people. Your descendants will be as many as the dust on the ground on which you lay."

When Jacob woke up he was amazed. "This is truly a holy place," he said. "It must be the very house of God and gate of heaven!"

Taking the stone on which he had rested his head during the night, Jacob set it up as a pillar, and poured oil over it.

He named the place Bethel, which means "house of God". Then he made a solemn promise to God. "If the God of my fathers stays with me and keeps me safe, then he shall be my God, too."

Jacob went to live among his mother's people. He had two wives – Rachel and Leah – who gave him twelve sons, and he became very rich. After many years he and his family returned

DID YOU KNOW?
The idea of a 'stairway to heaven' comes from Jacob's dream.

to Canaan. The night before he crossed into the Promised Land, Jacob spent the night alone in prayer. A stranger appeared and wrestled with him all night.

"What is your name?" asked the stranger eventually. Jacob told him. "From now on your name shall be Israel." Jacob realised he had been wrestling with God.

The next day Jacob was finally reunited with his brother, Esau.

Joseph's wonderful coat
Genesis 37:1–11

Of all his sons, Jacob loved Joseph, the second to youngest, the best.

When Joseph was seventeen, Jacob gave him a special coat to wear. It was woven with many colours and had long sleeves: the kind of coat that only a privileged, eldest son might own.

When Joseph's brothers saw how their father spoiled him, they were very jealous of Joseph and began to hate their younger brother.

Joseph used to have wonderful dreams, and he always knew what they meant. One day he told his brothers about his latest dream. "I dreamed that we were tying up sheaves of wheat that we had harvested. My sheaf stood up tall and straight, but all your sheaves bowed down to mine."

"Does this mean you think you are going to rule over us?" cried his brothers, and they were so furious with him that they could not speak to him again.

Joseph had a second dream, similar to the first; this time he saw the sun, the moon and eleven stars all bowing down to him.

When he told his father about it, Jacob scolded him. "That's a fine dream to have!" he said. "Do you really think that one day your mother and I, and all your brothers, will bow down to you?" But the old man kept the dream in his mind.

Joseph becomes a slave

Genesis 37:12–36

One day Jacob sent Joseph to visit his brothers, who were far away up in the mountains with the sheep. While he was still a long way off, they saw him coming, wearing his colourful new coat.

"Here comes the dreamer," they said. "Let's kill him and throw his body into a pit. We can say he was caught by a wild animal."

"No," said Reuben, the eldest. "Let's just throw him into a pit and leave him to die." He didn't want to kill Joseph, but planned to come back later and rescue him.

When Joseph arrived, they grabbed him, took off his coat, and tossed him down into an empty well. Then they sat down to eat.

While they were having their meal, some merchants came along. Their camels were laden with spices and goods that the merchants hoped to sell in Egypt. One of Joseph's brothers had an idea.

"Let's sell Joseph to these merchants," he said, "then we won't have to kill him. After all, he is our brother." The others agreed. They hauled Joseph out of the well and sold him as a slave to the merchants for twenty pieces of silver.

Before returning home, the brothers dipped Joseph's coat in goat's blood. "Look what we've found, Father!" they cried, when they saw Jacob. "Isn't this the coat you gave Joseph?"

Jacob was horrified. "Yes, it's Joseph's coat! Some wild animal must have killed him!" And nothing anyone could say comforted him. He would grieve for Joseph for the rest of his life.

But Joseph was not dead – he was on his way to Egypt and God was looking after him.

DID YOU KNOW?
At this time, the people of Egypt traded not with money, but with goods, livestock or even their own labour. Slavery was rare.

Joseph in prison
Genesis 39:1–40:23

Joseph was sold at the slave market to a man called Potiphar, who was an important officer in charge of the Royal Guard at the palace of the Pharaoh, or king.

Joseph became so good at his job that Potiphar put him in charge of his household. Then one day Potiphar's wife told her husband lies about Joseph, and Potiphar had him thrown into prison.

The keeper of the prison soon discovered that Joseph was special, too: he put him in charge of the other prisoners. Among them were the Pharaoh's butler and baker. One morning the two men told Joseph that they had each had a strange dream.

"My God has made me wise," said Joseph. "Describe your dreams and I will tell you what they mean."

"In my dream," said the butler, "I saw a grapevine with three bunches of grapes on it. I squeezed them into Pharaoh's wine cup and gave it to him to drink."

"The three bunches are three days," said Joseph. "In three days Pharaoh will forgive you and you will be serving him with wine again."

"In my dream," said the baker, "I was carrying three baskets of delicious pastries to Pharaoh. But some birds flew down and pecked at them."

"I'm afraid it means that in three days you will die," said Joseph.

It was Pharaoh's birthday in three days' time. Just as Joseph had said, Pharaoh had the baker put to death and gave the butler back his job. Happy, the butler returned to his work and forgot all about Joseph.

DID YOU KNOW?

The American term for prison – 'penitentiary' – comes from the medieval Latin word penitentiaria, which means 'penance'. Penance is when a person accepts punishment for crimes or sins they have committed.

Joseph the ruler of Egypt
Genesis 41:1–45

Joseph remained in prison for another two years. Then one night Pharaoh himself had a strange dream. He dreamed he stood by a river. Seven fat cows came out of the water and ate the grass in the meadow. Then seven thin cows came out of the water. They ate up the seven fat cows, but stayed as thin as before!

None of Pharaoh's wise men and advisers could tell him what the dream meant. Suddenly, his butler remembered Joseph and told Pharaoh. Joseph was immediately brought from prison.

"I hear you are wise and can interpret dreams," said Pharaoh.

"My God speaks through me," said Joseph, "and tells me what to say."

So Pharaoh described his dream. After thinking about it for a little while, Joseph told him what it meant.

"God has shown you the future, Pharaoh," he said. "There will be seven 'fat' years with plenty of food for everyone. Then there will be seven 'thin' years without rain, when everyone will be hungry. During the years of plenty, you should store all the grain from the harvest carefully so that there will be enough to last during the years of famine."

Pharaoh was very impressed with Joseph. "Your God has indeed filled you with wisdom," he said, and he gave Joseph the

highest office in the land, second only to Pharaoh himself. Joseph was given rich clothes to wear and Pharaoh's own ring. He travelled through the country in his own chariot and everywhere he went, people bowed down before him.

DID YOU KNOW?
Pharaohs reigned over Egypt for 3,000 years. The last Pharaoh to rule was Cleopatra VII, from 51 BC to 30 BC. Following her death, Egypt fell under the rule of the Romans.

Joseph sees his family again
Genesis 41–47

For seven years, there was plenty of food. Joseph was put in charge of making sure that grain was stored carefully all over Egypt. Then came seven years without rain. Many regions went hungry, but not Egypt, and soon people started travelling to Egypt to buy food. Amongst them were Joseph's elder brothers.

Joseph knew them at once. But they did not recognise him.

Joseph accused them of being spies. They assured him they were not, but Joseph kept one brother as a prisoner and told the others to return home and fetch their youngest brother, to prove that their story was true. It was just a trick so that Joseph could see his brother Benjamin again.

DID YOU KNOW?
The Ancient Egyptians called their ancestors akhu, which means 'shining ones'. Golden stars were used to represent them in decorations on tombs and temples.

The next time the brothers came to Egypt, they brought Benjamin with them. Joseph hid a silver cup inside the bag that Benjamin carried. Then, when the brothers tried to leave the palace, he had them arrested. Benjamin was ordered to remain in Egypt as a slave. "That would break our father Jacob's heart," said the brothers. "Take one of us instead."

Joseph could not hide his secret from them any longer. Overcome with tears of joy, he told his brothers who he was, and begged them to hurry home to fetch their father, Jacob.

So it was that Jacob and his whole family came to live in Egypt, joyfully reunited with Joseph. The people of God lived in Egypt for many years, and Jacob's twelve sons eventually became the ancestors of the twelve tribes of Israel.

Baby Moses
Exodus 1:15–2:9

The people of God – the Israelites – lived in comfort in Egypt for many years. Their numbers grew and some of them became very rich and important. But all this changed when a new Pharaoh, who was afraid of the Israelites, came to rule Egypt.

He made all the Israelites become slaves and put them to work making bricks and roads. He also ordered that any new boy child born to an Israelite woman should be killed. At this time, it seemed as if God had deserted his people.

One woman managed to save her son by putting him in a basket woven from bulrushes, which she hid among the reeds at the edge of the river. Her little daughter, Miriam stayed nearby to watch.

Before long, Pharaoh's daughter came down to the river to bathe. She saw the basket in the reeds and sent her maid to fetch it. The princess realised the crying infant must be a slave baby and she felt sorry for him.

DID YOU KNOW?
Some believe the name Moses means 'out of the water'. "She named him Moses, 'Because,' she said, 'I drew him out of the water'. " **(Exodus 2:10)**

Then Miriam came forward. "He's hungry," she said to the princess. "Would you like me to fetch a slave woman to nurse him for you?" The princess thought that was a good idea and so Miriam fetched her mother.

The princess paid the slave woman to nurse the child, and so the baby was brought up by his own mother.

When he was older, Pharaoh's daughter adopted him and called him Moses. He went to live in the palace and was taught to read and write like other royal children.

But Moses never forgot the God of his ancestors and the teachings of his real mother.

God calls Moses
Exodus 2:11–4:17

Although he grew up in a palace, Moses knew that his people suffered greatly at the hands of the Egyptians and it made him very angry. One day he saw an Egyptian guard hitting a slave. Moses was so angry; he killed the guard and then had to flee for his own life.

He escaped into the desert of Midian, where he became a shepherd for a holy man called Jethro. During this time, Pharaoh died and God heard the people of Egypt crying out to be saved from their slavery.

One day, Moses was leading Jethro's sheep in search of water in the desert, when he came to the holy mountain of Sinai. There, Moses noticed a bush that seemed to be on fire, yet it did not burn away. He went to take a closer look, and suddenly the voice of God spoke: "Moses, do not come any nearer. Take off your sandals, for this is holy ground. I am the God of your ancestors, the God of Abraham, the God of Isaac and the God of Jacob."

Moses knelt and covered his face, he was so afraid.

"I have seen the suffering of my people and heard their prayers for help," God said, "and I want you to go back to Egypt to set them free. Tell them I sent you."

"But what if they won't listen to me?" asked Moses. "What if they don't believe you have sent me?"

"Throw your staff on the ground," said God. Moses did as God asked. Immediately the staff turned into a snake and Moses leaped back in fear. "Pick it up by the tail," said God. Moses did so and it turned back into a staff. "With this," said God, "you will convince them that the Lord God of their fathers has really sent you."

DID YOU KNOW?
Exodus is the second book of the Bible and is a part of the Pentateuch, which is the name given to the first five books of the Old Testament: Genesis, Exodus, Leviticus, Numbers and Deuteronomy.

Moses the leader
Exodus 5–11

God gave Moses the courage to go back to Egypt and tell Pharaoh to release the Israelites. Pharaoh refused and instead, to spite Moses, he made the slaves work harder than ever before.

Moses warned him that Egypt would suffer plagues, or disasters, if he did not let the Israelites go, but Pharaoh continued to ignore Moses, and so the plagues came.

First the river turned into blood, killing all the fish and making the water smell terrible. Then the whole of Egypt was plagued by swarms of frogs.

Pharaoh remained stubborn.

Next came gnats, then flies, then disease, which killed all the livestock, and boils, which caused misery for everyone. The seventh plague was hailstorms that flattened the crops, followed by locusts that turned the sky black and ate every green leaf that remained.

Still Pharaoh remained stubborn and refused to free the Israelites from slavery.

For three days darkness covered the land. Everyone knew these were signs from God, but Pharaoh refused to do as Moses asked.

Finally, Moses promised a plague more terrible than all the others. At midnight, all the first-born children and animals in the land would die – including Pharaoh's own son. Only the children of God's chosen people would be spared from this final, terrible, plague.

DID YOU KNOW?

An ancient water trough found in El Arish, bearing hieroglyphics detailing a period of darkness, is just one archaeological find that may prove the occurrence of the ten plagues of Egypt.

The first Passover
Exodus 12:1–42

God told Moses exactly what the Israelites must do to ensure that the angel of death did not visit them that night. Each household had to kill a lamb and roast it with herbs. Everyone should eat quickly, standing up, dressed and ready to escape into the desert. They should eat the meat with unleavened bread (that is, made without yeast) and smear some of the blood from the lamb on the doorposts of their homes. The angel would pass over all those houses marked in this way.

The Israelites were to keep this day, which would be known as the Passover, a holy feast in honour of the Lord, every year, forever more.

The Israelites did as Moses had told them.

At midnight, the angel of the Lord passed over the land and took the lives of all the firstborn in each household. Not one house was spared. But the angel passed by the Israelite houses marked with blood, just as the Lord had promised.

Pharaoh, overcome with grief at the death of his son – the heir to the throne of Egypt – summoned Moses to him in the middle of the night and ordered him to take the slaves, together with all their sheep and cattle, and leave Egypt as soon as they could.

And so, after four hundred and thirty years of slavery, the Hebrews took all their belongings and walked out of Egypt and into the desert, with Moses leading them and the Lord guiding his people with a pillar of cloud.

DID YOU KNOW?

According to the Bible, 600,000 men – not counting women and children – left Egypt after God sent the plagues.

Escape from Pharaoh
Exodus 13:17–15:21

God led his chosen people through the desert towards the Red Sea. By day they followed the pillar of cloud, and at night they followed a pillar of fire, so the people were never left to lose their way.

Meanwhile, Pharaoh changed his mind. "What have I done allowing the Hebrews to leave my service?" he asked. Furious, he sent out his army to recapture the slaves and bring them back for punishment.

When they saw the dust cloud caused by the galloping horses and chariots behind them, and the Red Sea in front of them, the Israelites were terrified. They accused Moses of leading them to their deaths.

"Do not be afraid!" said Moses. "The Lord God will keep us safe!"

Moses stretched out his hand over the sea. A fierce wind arose and drove back the sea to right and left, leaving a channel of dry land. The people hurried across.

Pharaoh's army saw the channel through the Red Sea and galloped after them. Suddenly, the wind dropped and the waters rolled back, trapping the Egyptians in the mud and waves. No one escaped.

That day, the people sang songs and danced in honour of the Lord God:

Sing of the Lord: he has covered himself in glory.
Horse and rider he has thrown into the sea!

DID YOU KNOW?
The Red Sea may have been given its name because of a type of bacterial algae that grows there, which makes the water appear red when it blooms.

DID YOU KNOW?
A gold chest was made for the tablets on which Moses wrote the Ten Commandments. It was called the Ark of the Covenant.

Moses the law-giver

Exodus 20:1–24

Moses led the people to the mountain of Sinai, where God had first spoken to him. Here, God gave Moses two stone slabs on which were the laws by which his chosen people were to live their lives.

On the first stone were the laws concerning their duty to God. They must not worship other gods. They must not worship idols of wood or stone. They must keep God's name holy. They must keep God's day – the Sabbath – holy. And they must honour their parents.

The second tablet contained the laws concerning their duty to each other. They must not kill. They must not be unfaithful to their wife or husband. They must not steal anything. They must not tell lies. They must not be envious of another person.

These were the Ten Commandments that God gave to his chosen people through Moses. On Sinai, God made a solemn agreement – a covenant – with his people: they were to promise to live by these commandments, and God in turn would promise to be their God, and they his chosen people for all time.

The story of Ruth
Ruth 1:1–4:18

There was a Jewish widow living in Moab, called Naomi. She had lived there with her husband and two sons who had both married Moabite women. Her husband and sons were dead, and Naomi longed to return to her own country.

Her daughter-in-law, Ruth, decided to go with her. "I want your home to be my home," said Ruth, "and your God to be my God."

The two women came to Bethlehem, where they made their home near land owned by Boaz, a relative of Naomi's husband.

Each day Ruth went out into the fields and picked up the stalks of corn left behind after the harvest, to feed herself and Naomi. One day Boaz himself noticed her.

"Who is this young woman?" he asked his servant. "Does she belong to anyone?"

"She is the Moabite woman who came back with Naomi after her husband died." The servant told Boaz just how hard Ruth worked.

Boaz was impressed with Ruth and so he instructed his reapers to leave extra corn in Ruth's path, and told her to stay in his own fields, where she would be safe.

Ruth fell on her knees and thanked him.

"I know of your kindness to your mother-in-law," said Boaz. "And how you left your own mother and father to care for her. May the Lord God reward you."

In time, Boaz took Ruth to be his wife and the Lord blessed her with a son whom they called Obed.

Obed would become the father of Jesse – the father of David.

DID YOU KNOW?
Only two books of the Bible are named after women; Ruth is one, the other is Esther.

The call of Samuel

1 Samuel 3:1–10

One day a woman named Hannah brought her son Samuel to the temple at Shiloh, where the Ark of the Covenant was kept. She left him with Eli, the priest in charge. For many years Hannah had longed for a child and had promised God that if he gave her a baby, she would give him to the temple, to serve God.

One night, when Samuel lay sleeping, he was woken by a voice calling: "Samuel! Samuel!" He thought it was Eli calling, so he ran to see what Eli wanted.

"I did not call you, my son. Go back to bed," said Eli. But Samuel heard the voice again, and again he ran to Eli. The third time it happened Eli realised that it was God calling the boy.

"If you hear the voice again," he told Samuel, "say 'Speak, Lord. Your servant is listening.'"

Samuel did just as Eli had told him. From that moment, God spoke to Samuel. And as he grew up, all God's people knew that he was God's prophet – his special messenger – and honoured him.

DID YOU KNOW?
The name Samuel means 'heard of God' or 'asked of God'. Eli means 'high' or 'my God'.

Samuel chooses a king
1 Samuel 9:1–15:35

The people of God had a very strong enemy at this time: the Philistines. They attacked the Israelites and tried to take over the Promised Land. Some of the elders went to Samuel and asked him to choose a king to lead them into battle. Samuel asked God for advice.

"Do as they ask," said the Lord God. "It is me they have rejected, not you. They no longer want me to lead them. But you must tell them exactly what it means to have a king."

Samuel went back to the elders and explained to them that a king would take their sons and make them serve as soldiers in his army. He would take their daughters to work for him, the best of their land and a tenth of their flocks. But the people still insisted on having a king so they could be like other nations.

So Samuel chose a handsome young man called Saul. He consecrated Saul to the service of God by anointing him with holy oil, and proclaimed him king.

In a very short time, Saul raised an army and fought well against the Philistines. But he became proud and hard. He broke important religious laws and refused to obey Samuel.

"Since you have rejected God," said Samuel, "so God has rejected you as king."

Samuel never saw Saul again. Instead, he went under God's guidance to find a new king for the chosen people.

DID YOU KNOW?
A theocracy is a society that is ruled in accordance with the law of God, usually by officials of religious status, such as priests.

Samuel and David
1 Samuel 16:1–13

Samuel was upset by Saul's disobedience and often, when he thought about Saul, his eyes would fill with tears. When God saw Samuel weeping for Saul, he asked, "How long will you mourn for Saul? You know I have rejected him and he will not be king."

Then God told Samuel to fill his horn with oil and sent him to the town of Bethlehem. A farmer named Jesse lived there, and God had chosen one of Jesse's sons to be the next king.

At first, Samuel was afraid to go. "If Saul hears of this, he will kill me," he said.

Samuel arrived in Bethlehem and ordered a feast in honour of the Lord God. It was an exciting occasion, and everyone attended including Jesse and all his family.

One by one, Jesse introduced each of his seven sons to Samuel. They were all tall, handsome young men, and as he met each one Samuel thought, "Surely this young man must be God's choice!"

But every time a voice inside Samuel's head said, "No, not this one." It was very puzzling.

"Are these all your sons?" he asked Jesse.

"Except for David, my youngest," said Jesse. "He's looking after the sheep."

Samuel said they couldn't begin the feast until David arrived. They sent for the young man, and he arrived looking bright, handsome and fit.

"This is the one I have chosen," said God to Samuel. "Anoint him king!"

Samuel anointed David with holy oil in front of his

brothers. He would be king of Israel one day, but in the meantime he was to return to his sheep. From that moment, the spirit of the Lord was close to David.

DID YOU KNOW?
It was common for the youngest son of a farmer to be given the job of shepherd, whilst his older, stronger brothers would help with more strenuous tasks.

David and his harp

1 Samuel 16:14–23

David loved to play the harp and sing while he spent lonely days and nights watching over his sheep, and he became famous for his songs.

King Saul at this time was very ill. He suffered from fits of madness and depression which only music could soothe. His servants told him he should send for a skilled musician, someone who could play for him whenever he had one of these attacks of illness, and so bring him relief. "Find me such a man!" said Saul.

One of the king's soldiers told them about Jesse's son, David. He was not only a good musician, but he had courage and was a man of God.

Messengers were sent to Jesse from the king, asking that David should come and play for the king.

And so whenever King Saul needed him, David left his flocks to come and play sweet, gentle music to soothe the king's madness. King Saul came to love this young man from Bethlehem who was able to bring peace and calm to his troubled mind.

David and Goliath

1 Samuel 17:1-51

Three of David's brothers were soldiers in King Saul's army. One morning, Jesse sent David out to them with supplies of food. He reached his brothers in time to see a giant of a man – over three metres tall – step from the ranks of the Philistine army. Goliath challenged the Israelites to send out a champion to fight him in single combat and finish the war quickly.

The soldiers of King Saul were terrified of him.

"I'll go and fight him!" said David. But King Saul would not allow it, saying David was only a boy.

David told Saul about the times he had killed a lion and a bear while guarding his sheep. God had helped him then, and he would help him now. Reluctantly, Saul allowed him to take up Goliath's challenge.

David refused to wear armour or carry a sword. Instead, he went down to the river and picked out five smooth stones, which he put in his shepherd's pouch. With his sling in his hand, he went to face Goliath. Goliath roared with laughter and scorned such a small champion. David put a stone in his sling. He whirled the sling around his head and the stone struck Goliath on the forehead, knocking him out. David then took Goliath's own sword and cut off the giant's head.

When the Philistines saw their champion was dead, they fled.

DID YOU KNOW?
Shepherds used to carry a slingshot at all times, in order to throw stones at animals that threatened their flocks.

David in hiding

1 Samuel 24:1–22

David became a fine soldier and King Saul made him commander of his army. He was handsome, brave and popular and the people sang his praises instead of praising Saul. He was also a close friend of the king's son, Jonathan, and Saul grew mad with jealousy.

One day the king suddenly threw his spear at David. It missed its target, but David had to flee for his life. From then on, David had to hide from the king and his men, who searched everywhere for David, to kill him.

DID YOU KNOW?
During the war with Palestine, Saul did not believe Samuel would arrive in time to carry out a sacrifice, so he did it himself. This displeased God as it showed Saul's lack of faith.

One night, in the cave where David was hiding, Saul and his guard came to rest. David would not harm Saul, but while they slept, he cut off a piece of Saul's robe. When dawn came, David followed Saul out of the cave and showed him the piece of cloth.

"My lord king," he said, "I could have killed you, but I am your loyal servant. Why do you want to kill me?" Saul was overcome with grief, but not for long.

Soon after, Saul went to war with the Philistines again. This time he was wounded and his three sons were slain. When he saw that the Philistines had won the battle and his sons were dead, Saul killed himself.

When David heard of their deaths, he was very sad.

David the king

2 Samuel 5:1–10

Now that Saul was dead, David could return to his own land. His own tribe of Judah made him their king, as Samuel had anointed him when he was a boy. Saul's remaining sons ruled in the north. But in time they died too, and so David became king over all the tribes of Israel. When the Philistines heard the news, they marched against him, but David defeated them in battle. Never again did they attack the people of God.

David conquered other lands, too, and made a great kingdom. He needed a capital city and chose a strong fortress called Jerusalem, set high on a hill in the middle of the kingdom. But he had to take it from the Jebusites who lived there, and refused to let him enter the gates.

David sent some men secretly into the tunnel that ran under the wall of the city, carrying the water supply. They came up inside the city and opened the gates so David and his army could take the Jebusites by surprise.

Jerusalem became David's city.

Jerusalem, city of God

2 Samuel 6:1–15

King David had captured the fortress of Jerusalem and made it the capital city of his kingdom. This is where he had his court, and where he ruled over Israel.

But David wanted Jerusalem to be God's city, too, where God might live among his chosen people. So he decided that the sacred Ark of the Covenant, that held the sacred stone tablets on which were written the commandments of God, should be brought to Jerusalem. While the Ark was with them, the people knew that God was with them, too.

David sent for the Ark and it was brought to the city in a great procession of rejoicing people. Musicians played and David was so happy that he threw off his royal robes and joined in the dancing with everyone else. He just wanted to give praise and glory to God.

The Ark was carried to a special tent, where it would remain until a temple could be built for it.

So the city of Jerusalem became the city of God.

DID YOU KNOW?

David was not only an accomplished warrior, but also a great writer. Many believe that it was David who wrote most, if not all, of the book of Psalms.

Solomon's dream
1 Kings 3:5–15

When he grew old, King David chose his son Solomon to be king after him. Solomon was anointed king just before David died.

Although David had given him a great deal of advice,

once his father was dead Solomon realised just how difficult it would be to rule a kingdom by himself.

Like David, Solomon had a great love for God, so he went to the holy place at Gibeon where he offered sacrifices to God and prayed for guidance.

During the night, God appeared to him in a dream.

"Ask me for what you want most, and I will give it to you," said God to Solomon.

Solomon replied, "You have chosen me to be king, Lord, after my father David. You showed him great mercy when he followed your ways. Now you have brought me to the throne. But I am young and inexperienced, and I am king over a great nation. Give me, therefore, a wise heart so that I can be a good ruler for your people."

God was very pleased with Solomon's answer. "You could have asked for a long life, or riches, or success over your enemies, but instead you have asked for wisdom. I will do as you ask. I am therefore giving you a wise and understanding heart so that you will be a good king. You will be unique. There is no one to compare with you before, or will there be anyone after your death. And because you asked for wisdom, I will also give you those things you didn't ask for: a long life, riches, and victory over your enemies. Just keep my commandments, like your father, and I will give you all these things."

Solomon became a wise king. Over three thousand of his clever sayings – called proverbs – were written into books by the skilled writers of his court, and, in addition, Solomon wrote many songs and poems. He became famous among his people for his wisdom and knowledge, especially of the natural world, and his fame spread to other lands. Many people came from around the world to ask his advice and bring him gifts.

Solomon the wise
1 Kings 3:16–28

One day, two women came to Solomon's court with a baby boy.

One of them said, "My lord, this woman and I live in the same house. I gave birth to a baby boy. There was no one else in the house at the time. Then, this woman's baby died one night, so she came to my room, took my baby while I was asleep and put her dead baby in its place. When I woke to feed the baby I knew at once that it wasn't my child."

DID YOU KNOW?
The phrase 'the judgement of Solomon' refers to this story, and is used to describe a situation in which someone has judged a matter with wisdom and insight.

"No! That's not right!" said the other woman. "This baby is mine. The dead child was hers!"

Solomon turned to his officer. "Fetch me a sword," he said. When the sword was brought, he said, "Now, cut the child in half, and give half to each woman."

The woman who was the child's real mother threw herself at the king's feet. "Please, my lord," she begged him, "give the child to her. Do not kill him."

But the other woman said, "The baby won't belong to either of us. Cut him up."

Solomon made his decision. "Give the child to the first woman. She is his real mother."

The whole of Israel came to hear of this story, and everyone recognised that God had indeed blessed Solomon with great wisdom.

The temple of Solomon
1 Kings 6:1–38

David had brought the sacred Ark of the Covenant to Jerusalem. Now his son Solomon started work on a beautiful temple, four years after he became king.

Builders came from Phoenicia. Cedar, cypress and juniper wood were brought by sea. Blocks of special stone were cut from the mountains. Gold and silver came from other lands. Thousands upon thousands of workers were employed.

The huge doors were made of bronze. Walls were made of cedar wood, carved with flowers and trees. Altars were made of cedar wood and covered in gold. The inner temple, the holy of holies where the Ark of the Covenant was to be kept, was entirely covered in gold.

It took seven years for the temple of Jerusalem to be finished. At last, in solemn procession, the priests of Levi carried the sacred chest from the tent to the holy of holies. As they left, a cloud filled the temple, so thick that the priests were unable to continue the service. It was the glory of the Lord God.

King Solomon turned to face the people. In the hush, he told them that God had come to dwell among them in the temple. Then he led them in a great prayer that God would always bless his house and his people who worshipped him there.

God appeared to Solomon a second time.

"I grant your prayer," he said, "and I consecrate this temple you have built. My eyes and my heart shall always be here. If you walk with me and keep my commandments, I shall make your royal throne secure over Israel, just as I promised David your father. But if you turn away from me,

and worship other gods, then I will cut Israel off from the land I have given them, and leave the temple for ever."

Elijah in the desert

1 Kings 16:29–17:24

When Ahab became king of Israel his wife, Jezebel, brought from her own country hundreds of priests of Baal, and set about executing all the prophets of the Lord God she could find.

As a result of their wickedness, God sent his prophet, Elijah, to warn King Ahab that there would be a drought in Israel lasting many years.

After delivering his message, Elijah had to hide in the desert, to escape from Jezebel. Each day ravens brought him bread and meat to eat and he drank from a brook, Cherith, east of the River Jordan.

DID YOU KNOW?
The name Jezebel is now sometimes used when referring to a cruel woman or one of low morals.

When the brook dried up, God sent Elijah to the city of Sidon.

At the city gates, Elijah met a widow gathering sticks. He asked her for a drink of water and some food.

"As the Lord God lives, I have no bread," said the woman, "but only a handful of flour in a jar and a little oil in a jug. I shall make my son and myself a last meal, and then we will both die."

"Don't be afraid," said Elijah. "Cook your meal, but bring some for me as well, and you will find that the jar of flour will never be used up, or the jug of oil emptied, until this drought comes to an end."

There was not only enough food for them all, but also the flour and oil never ran out, just as Elijah had promised.

Then the widow's son became very ill and died. "Why have you allowed my son to be taken from me?" she demanded of Elijah. Elijah took the boy and prayed over him, and after a while he came back to life.

Overjoyed, the widow said, "Now I know that you truly are a man of God and the word of God that you speak is truth."

Elijah and the prophets of Baal
1 Kings 18:20–38

The drought in Israel lasted three years. Then Elijah returned to King Ahab and challenged him to prove that Baal was a greater god than the Lord God of Israel.

"Tell all the people of Israel, and the four hundred and fifty prophets of Baal, to meet me on Mount Carmel," he said to Ahab.

There, he ordered them to prepare an altar and sacrifice to Baal while he built an altar to God. But they were not to set fire to it yet.

"Let he who is the true God set fire to the wood," said Elijah.

When their altar was complete, the prophets of Baal prayed to their god to bring fire for them. For hours they cried out to Baal and danced round and round their altar. But no voice answered them, and no fire lit their wood. Elijah laughed at them. "Cry louder," he said. "Perhaps your god is asleep. Shout louder to wake him."

Elijah built his own altar out of twelve stones – one for each tribe of Israel – covered it with wood and dug a deep trench round it. He prepared his sacrifice and put it on the altar. Then he told the people to pour water over the altar until it was all completely soaked and water filled the trench.

"God of Abraham, Isaac and Jacob," he prayed, "send fire, so that your people will know that you are God in Israel and that I am your servant."

Instantly, the soaking wood burst into flames. The wood, stones and the offering on the altar – even the water in the trench around it – were completely burned up by the fire.

When the people saw this, they fell down and worshipped God. And rain came again to Israel: the drought was over.

DID YOU KNOW?
There were two men in the Old Testament who never died. Instead, God took them straight into heaven. They were called Enoch and Elijah.

The story of Jonah
Jonah

Jonah was a prophet who didn't really want to do what God asked of him. When God said, "Go to the city of Nineveh and persuade the people to change their wicked ways," Jonah ran off in the opposite direction and boarded a sailing ship going far away. But God sent a violent storm to toss the ship about. Jonah told the terrified sailors that he had probably made God angry.

"Throw me into the sea," said Jonah, "and the storm will die down." The sailors reluctantly threw Jonah over the side of the ship and immediately the wind dropped.

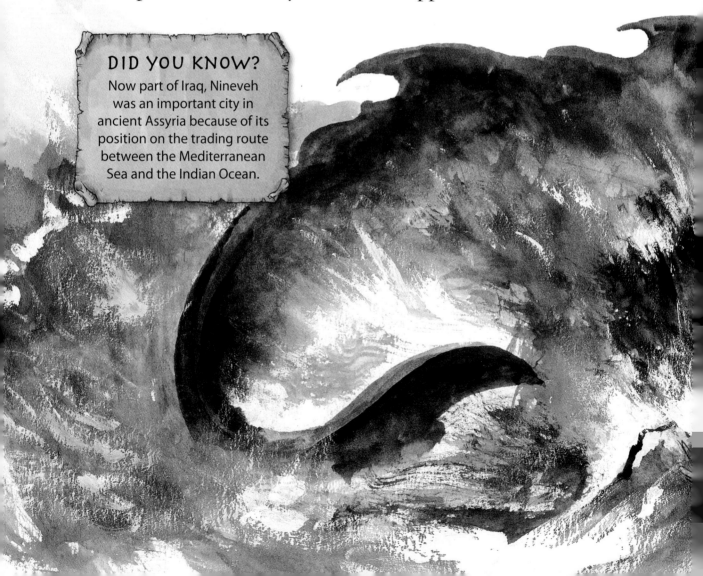

DID YOU KNOW?
Now part of Iraq, Nineveh was an important city in ancient Assyria because of its position on the trading route between the Mediterranean Sea and the Indian Ocean.

Then God commanded a big fish to swallow Jonah, and after three days and nights the big fish spewed him safely on to a beach. Jonah immediately thanked God for saving his life. "Now go to Nineveh with my message!" said God. The people listened to Jonah and were sorry for their wicked ways, so God forgave them.

Jonah was angry that God should show mercy to these people. He sat down under a tree and sulked, but overnight the tree shrivelled up. Jonah felt sorry for it.

God said to him, "Jonah, you feel sorry for this tree that meant nothing to you. Won't you let me feel sorry for all the people of Nineveh?" In this way, God showed that his love was for people of all nations, not just the people of Israel.

Stories of the Prophets

Throughout history, God chose men and women to speak for him and pass on his messages to the people about things that were going to happen. These were the 'prophets'. They were not always clever, rich or gifted: very often they did not want to be God's messengers at all, because they knew that they would be unpopular. But God always gave them the strength and gifts they needed to do his work.

Jeremiah
Jeremiah 18:1–19:15

Jeremiah was a quiet, gentle young man. He came from a priestly family that lived near Jerusalem. When God called him to be a prophet, Jeremiah knew the task would be difficult and was worried he would not know how to speak his Lord's words to the masses.

So God touched Jeremiah's mouth and said, "I have put my words into your mouth. Today I have put you in charge over nations and kingdoms, to uproot and knock down, to destroy and overthrow, to build and to plant."

He sent Jeremiah to a potter's house. There he saw the potter making a clay pot. When the pot lost its shape the potter wet the clay, made it into a ball once more and started again. This time the pot was perfect.

DID YOU KNOW?
Potters are important in the Bible because they are symbolic of God's creation, just as shepherds are symbolic of God's watchful care of his followers.

God told Jeremiah that the people were like clay in his hands. If they continued to live wickedly he would destroy them. But if they kept his commandments and were sorry for what they had done wrong, he would make them good and strong.

Jeremiah went to the priests and wise men of Israel and held up a pottery jar for them to see. Then he smashed it to the ground, breaking it into small pieces. "This is what will happen to the people of Judah," he said, "if they do not listen to the word of the Lord!"

Jeremiah in prison

Jeremiah 38:1–13

Jeremiah's warnings were ignored, and before long, as he had promised, Jerusalem was captured by the army of Babylon. The people rebelled, but Jeremiah warned them to leave the city: disaster was coming!

The city leaders hated the prophet. He was arrested and thrown into a dark, underground prison. Then they went to the king and demanded that Jeremiah should be put to death. "Do what you want with him," said the cowardly king.

They were afraid to kill a man of God. Instead, they lowered Jeremiah into a deep well. He sank into the soft mud at the bottom and was left to die.

DID YOU KNOW?
Like today, there was very little rainfall in the Middle East during biblical times, so wells were dug to enable people to draw water from deep in the ground.

One of the royal servants heard what had happened and told the king. "My lord king," he said, "these men have done a wicked thing. Jeremiah will starve." The king then gave the servant permission to rescue Jeremiah.

Taking thirty men to help him, he dropped some rags down to Jeremiah to put under his arms, and ropes to tie over them. Then they pulled Jeremiah out of the well.

Jeremiah was saved from death, but his words of warning from God were still ignored.

Exiles in Babylon

2 Chronicles 36:1–21

Just as the people disregarded Jeremiah's warnings, they also forgot the promises they had made when Josiah had been king, that they would keep to God's law.

Jerusalem was conquered by the invading armies of Babylon, ruled by King Nebuchadnezzar. They stole the temple treasures, knocked down the walls and burned the entire city to the ground. The people of Judah were marched into the city of Babylon.

Just as the prophet Isaiah had foretold, God's chosen people had lost their land, their holy city and their temple. Even their king was a prisoner. Despite the beauty of the city of Babylon, they were in a strange land and homesick. They made sad songs telling of their unhappiness:

We sat down by the waters of Babylon,
*   and we wept when we remembered Jerusalem.*
We hung our harps on the willow trees.

But they still had hope. God was with them, even in exile, and their king still lived. Through his prophets, Jeremiah and Ezekiel, God instructed his people to settle in Babylon and live according to his commandments. One day he would restore their fortunes and return them to the land of their fathers.

"The days are coming," said the Lord, "when I shall make a new covenant with my people. I shall forgive them and forget the things they have done wrong."

DID YOU KNOW?
Babylon was the capital city of Babylonia. In the ancient language of Akkadian, which was spoken in Mesopotamia at the time, 'Babylon' meant 'Gateway of the Gods'.

Daniel in the lions' den

Daniel 6:1–28

Daniel was a boy when the people of God were taken captive into Babylon. He grew up to be a good, wise young man, faithful to God, with a gift of being able to understand the meaning of dreams. It was this gift that brought him favour and rich rewards from the king, who made him ruler of the kingdom.

The other princes and nobles of Babylon were jealous of Daniel. They tricked the king into signing a new law that said no one could pray to any god except the king. Anyone caught disobeying this law would be thrown into the den of lions.

Three times a day, Daniel opened his window that faced Jerusalem, went down on his knees and prayed to the Lord God. It was easy for the officials to arrest him.

"We caught him praying to his God," they told the king. And although the king was deeply distressed, he had no choice but to give the order for Daniel to die. So Daniel was thrown into the den of lions.

That night, the king was unable to eat or sleep. As soon as it was light, he hurried to the lions' den. "Daniel!" he cried. "Has your God been able to save you from the lions?"

"May your majesty live for ever!" said Daniel, cheerfully. "My God sent his angel to seal the lions' jaws. They did me no harm."

The king ordered Daniel to be released, and sent a message all over his kingdom about the goodness of the God of Daniel: "He is the living God. His kingdom will last forever. He saves, sets free and works signs and wonders in the heavens and on the earth."

THE NEW TESTAMENT

The new covenant

The New Testament (an old word meaning covenant) is all about Jesus: God's own son. He is the one promised to the people through the prophets of the Old Testament: the new covenant between God and his people. It is made up of a number of accounts and letters written by the people who were close to Jesus, or who passed on his teachings.

The coming of the Romans

More than four hundred years passed after the last of the Old Testament prophets promised that God would send someone very special to make a new covenant with his people.

They were difficult times.

First, Greek conquerors took over the Promised Land from the Persians. A hero of the Jewish nation, Judas Maccabeus, fought the Greeks and brought a time of peaceful freedom for a while, but later the Romans conquered the Greeks and Palestine – the Promised Land – came under the Roman rule.

The Roman Empire was huge and powerful. Roman soldiers and officials were put in towns and cities to keep law and order and collect taxes. Everyone hated them.

The Jewish people longed for the day when a new king, or hero, would come and rescue them from Roman rule.

The Romans did not worship the God of the Jewish nation. When a Roman general named Pompey took over the city of Jerusalem, he marched into the temple to see what the Jewish God was like. He expected to see a huge statue, but instead it was quite empty.

The king chosen by the Romans to rule over the people of God at this time was a cruel, clever man called Herod the Great.

A baby for Elizabeth
Luke 1:5–25

In the days when Herod was king, there was a priest living in Judaea called Zechariah. He and his wife, Elizabeth, were faithful to God and obedient to his commandments. Their one sorrow was that despite all their prayers, they had not been blessed with children, and now they were both growing old.

One day, while Zechariah was serving in the temple and the people prayed outside, an angel appeared, standing by the altar. Zechariah was terrified.

"Do not be afraid," said the angel. "Your prayers have been heard. Your wife, Elizabeth, is to have a son and you must call him John. He will be a great joy to you both and he will bring a great deal of happiness and peace to the world. He will be great in the eyes of the Lord and through him many people will come back to God."

Zechariah found it hard to believe what the angel was saying.

"How can this be?" he asked. "We are old now. My wife is unable to have children."

"I am Gabriel," said the angel. "I come from God with this good news for you. Since you have not believed me, from now on you will be silent until all that I have said comes to pass."

When Zechariah came out of the sanctuary, he

could not tell anyone what had happened. The people were amazed: they realised he had seen a vision.

Just as the angel had promised, Elizabeth became pregnant. For five months she stayed quietly at home, rejoicing that the Lord God had blessed her in this way.

DID YOU KNOW?

Michaelmas day, on September 29th, is the feast day of St Michael. It is also known as the Feast of Saint Michael and All Angels.

Mary is chosen
Luke 1:26–38

God sent the angel Gabriel to Nazareth, a small town in Galilee. There he appeared to a young woman called Mary, who was engaged to be married to Joseph – a descendant of the family of King David.

"Rejoice, Mary," said Gabriel, "because the Lord is with you. You are the most blessed of all women!"

Mary was very troubled by this. She wondered what the angel's words could mean and why she should have such a special visitor.

"Do not be afraid, Mary," said Gabriel. "You have found favour with God. You will have a son and you must call him Jesus. He will be great. The son of the Most High. He will rule over the people of God and his reign will never end."

"How can this be?" asked Mary. "I am still a girl, and unmarried."

"The Holy Spirit will come to you," said the angel, "and God's power will cover you, so the child will be holy and called the Son of God. Know this as well, that your cousin, Elizabeth, is also going to have a son, even though she is old now. For nothing is impossible to God." Mary knelt down before the angel's feet and bowed her head. "I am God's faithful servant, and prepared to do whatever he asks of me," she said. "Let what you have said be done to me."

And when she looked up, the angel had gone.

DID YOU KNOW?

Whilst many Christians believe that angels are neither male nor female, artistic representations often show the archangel Gabriel in the form of a man.

Mary visits Elizabeth
Luke 1:39–56

After the angel had left, Mary went as quickly as she could to visit her cousin. As soon as Mary entered Zechariah's house and greeted Elizabeth, Elizabeth felt her baby leap for joy inside her womb. Suddenly, Elizabeth was filled with the Holy Spirit.

"Of all women, you are the most blessed!" she cried. "And blessed is the child you carry! As soon as I heard your voice, I felt my baby move inside me. How I am honoured that you have come to visit me."

Mary sang a great song of praise to God:

My soul sings of the greatness of the Lord and my spirit rejoices in God who is my Saviour.

Mary stayed with Elizabeth for three months, and then returned home.

The birth of John the Baptist
Luke 1:57–66

Soon afterwards, Elizabeth's baby was born. Just as the angel had promised, it was a boy. All Elizabeth's family and friends shared her happiness.

Now the time came to give the baby a name.

"His name is John," said Elizabeth.

"But no one in your family is called John!" argued Elizabeth's friends and family. They turned to Zechariah to see what he wanted to call his son. Zechariah was still unable to speak, so he wrote down instead.

"His name is John." And at that moment, Zechariah found he was able to speak again, and he gave great praise to God.

DID YOU KNOW?

Zechariah and Elizabeth went against the tradition of the time, which was to name a baby boy after his father.

Baby Jesus
Matthew 1:18–25

When Joseph discovered that Mary was expecting a child, he decided to quietly release her from her betrothal to him. But an angel came to him in a dream and told him not to be afraid to marry Mary. "The child is from God," said the angel, "and he will be called Jesus."

Now the Romans wanted to know just how many people lived in Palestine, so they could tax them. They ordered every Jewish man to go to his hometown to be registered and counted.

When Joseph arrived in his hometown of Bethlehem with Mary, it was crowded with people. They had travelled all the way from Nazareth and Mary was tired. Her baby was due to be born, and they had to find somewhere to rest for the night.

"Sorry, we haven't a room left," said the innkeeper. "You can go in the stable if you like. There's plenty of fresh straw."

So Joseph made a bed for Mary in the stable, and that night her son was born. She remembered what the angel had told her, and she called her baby Jesus.

Mary wrapped the baby Jesus in special strips of cloth, like bandages, called "swaddling". It made him feel very warm and secure. Jesus was put in one of the food mangers, where he slept on a bed of straw.

Jesus had been sent by God to save his people. The Saviour they all hoped for was born, not in a royal palace, but in a stable in Bethlehem.

The shepherds visit Jesus
Luke 2:8–21

The night Jesus was born, shepherds on the hillside above Bethlehem were watching over their sheep in the darkness. Suddenly, the sky above them filled with a dazzling light and an angel appeared. The shepherds were terrified. "Don't be afraid," said the angel. "I have great news for you and all people. Today in Bethlehem your Saviour has been born. You will find him lying in a manger, in a stable, wrapped in swaddling cloths."

Then the angel was joined by a great choir of angels, singing the praises of God:

Glory to God in the highest heaven,
And peace to those who have pleased him!

When the angels had gone, the shepherds looked at one another in amazement.

"What can this mean?" they said to each other. "Let us go down to Bethlehem and see for ourselves."

They hurried down to the town and just as the angel had told them, they found the stable where the newborn baby, wrapped in swaddling, was lying in a manger.

The shepherds were astonished. They told everybody what they had seen and heard, and Mary kept everything they said in her heart. Then the shepherds returned to their sheep, giving praise and glory to God.

Wise men from the East
Matthew 2:1–12

After Jesus was born, three wise men came to Jerusalem from the East, guided by a star. They were looking for the promised Messiah. As soon as they had seen the brilliant new star in the sky, they knew that this was the sign they had been waiting for.

"Where is the infant king of the Jews?" they asked everyone. "We have come to worship him. We have followed his star and have gifts for him."

When King Herod heard of the strangers looking for a king, he sent for them and listened to their story, pretending to be as deeply religious as they were and carefully concealing his anger and fear.

"Go to Bethlehem," he told them, "and when you have found the child come and let me know, so that I may go and pay him homage, too."

As the wise men left Jerusalem, the star they had seen appeared before them and led them to Bethlehem, to where Jesus and his parents were staying. They knew they had found the one they were looking for.

They knelt down in front of Jesus and gave him their gifts: gold for a king, frankincense for the worship of God, and myrrh – an oil used when burying the dead – to show the mortality of Jesus.

Afterwards, they returned home a different way. They had been warned in a dream not to go back to Herod, as he only wanted to kill Jesus.

It was the wise men that brought the good news of the Saviour to the world beyond Palestine.

DID YOU KNOW?
No one knows for sure how many wise men visited Jesus. We assume that there were three, because three gifts were given: gold, frankincense and myrrh.

The return to Nazareth
Matthew 2:13–23

When the wise men had left, Joseph was warned in a dream to take Mary and Jesus to Egypt, where they would be safe from King Herod. The king was furious that the wise men had deceived him. To make sure that there was no rival king to challenge him, Herod ordered his soldiers to kill every young boy under the age of two living in and around Bethlehem.

Not long after this, King Herod died. The angel returned to Joseph in another dream and told him it was safe to return to Israel.

Joseph took Mary and Jesus back home to Nazareth. They made their home there, with a workshop for Joseph's work as a carpenter.

So Jesus grew up, in a loving family devoted to God. Mary taught him all about his heavenly Father, through the stories and books of the Bible, and the traditional songs of praise and thanksgiving. Joseph took him to the temple for worship and taught him all about making things from wood, so he too could earn his living as a carpenter when he grew up.

As the boy Jesus grew older, he also grew in the knowledge and love of God. Everyone liked him, and God was pleased with him.

Jesus at the temple
Luke 2:41–52

Every year, Joseph, Mary and young Jesus went to Jerusalem to celebrate the feast of the Passover at the temple. It was an exciting, happy, family occasion.

When Jesus was twelve years old, they made the journey as usual, and when the time came to return home, Mary thought Jesus was with walking with friends and relatives. By the end of the day, however, it was clear that he was missing. She and Joseph returned to Jerusalem early next morning to look for him.

Three anxious days later, they found Jesus in the temple, talking to the priests and teachers and asking them questions. They were all astonished at how much he knew and understood.

"My child, how could you do this to us?" asked Mary. "We've been searching everywhere for you. We were so worried."

Jesus was surprised. "Why were you looking for me?" he asked. "Didn't you realise I'd be in my Father's house, doing his work?" But they didn't understand what he meant. So Jesus went home to Nazareth with them and stayed until it was the right time to start his important work for his heavenly Father.

DID YOU KNOW?
Every year, Jewish men had to travel to Jerusalem to attend religious festivals. Jesus would have made the long round trip from Nazareth to Jerusalem three times a year.

John the Baptist
Matthew 3:1–11

John was the cousin of Jesus. When John grew up he knew God wanted him to do some very important work for him. He made his home in the desert, wearing clothes made of rough camel hair tied with a leather belt, and living on locusts and wild honey. His only companions were the wild creatures of the desert.

Each day John went down to the banks of the River Jordan, where travellers would stop to refresh themselves and their animals, and spoke to them about God.

John was a wild-looking man and his words were stern, fierce and frightening. He warned the people that God was

angry with them. He said that they should be sorry for their evil ways and ask God to forgive them.

News of John spread far and wide. Here was a new prophet; someone sent by God with an important message for them. People flocked from all over the country to hear him preach. John baptised them in the river by dipping them under the water, as a sign that God had forgiven them.

He also told them of the Saviour that God was sending. "I am preparing the way for him," said John, "but I am not worthy enough to kneel and untie his sandals. I baptise you with water, but he will baptise you with the spirit of God."

Jesus is baptised

Mark 1:9–11

One day, Jesus came to be baptised by John. John knew immediately that this was the promised Saviour. "Here is the Lamb of God, who will take away the sins of the world!" he said.

Jesus had nothing to be sorry for because he had never disobeyed God, so John asked humbly, "Why do you come to me? It is I who should be baptised by you."

But Jesus said, "I believe this is what God wants."

So John baptised him. When Jesus came up out of the water, the spirit of God in the form of a dove flew down to him and the voice of God said, "This is My beloved Son, with whom I am well pleased."

"This is the man I spoke about," John said later. "I have seen him and I know he is God's Chosen One."

Not long after this, King Herod – son of the evil King Herod the Great – had John thrown into prison. He did not want to listen to John's message about asking God's forgiveness. Eventually, he had John put to death. Jesus was very sad when he heard the news. "A greater man than John has never lived," he said. "He was the herald, preparing the way for the kingdom of God."

Jesus is tempted
Luke 4:1–13

After Jesus had been baptised by John, he was led by the Holy Spirit into the desert to prepare himself, alone, for the tasks ahead. Jesus knew he had an important plan to carry out for his heavenly Father, so for forty days and nights he prayed to the Father for strength and guidance.

After so long without food, Jesus became exhausted and very hungry. It was then that Satan, the enemy of God, came to him.

"If you are really the Son of God," said Satan, "why don't you turn this stone into a loaf of bread and stop feeling hungry?"

But Jesus refused to use the power God had given him to satisfy his own need. "The Bible teaches us that we cannot live

on just bread," Jesus told Satan. "We need the word of God as well."

Then Satan took Jesus to a high place and showed him the whole world. "All this can be yours," he said, "if you will kneel and worship me!"

Jesus replied, "The first commandment is that we should worship the Lord our God and serve him alone."

Finally Satan took Jesus to the top of the temple in Jerusalem. "If you are the Son of God," he said, "throw yourself off this temple. The Bible says that God's angels will make sure you are not hurt!"

Jesus replied, "It also says that you must not put the Lord your God to the test!" And with that, Satan left.

Jesus visits Nazareth
Luke 4:16–30

Jesus left the desert and went down into Galilee, where he started to tell people all about God and how they should live their lives in order to please him.

One day he went into Nazareth, the town where he had grown up and worked as a carpenter.

It was the Sabbath, the holy day of the week, and he went to the synagogue with the other Jewish men. During the service, Jesus stood up to read and he was given the scroll of the prophet Isaiah. He opened it and read a passage that told of the coming of the Messiah, or Saviour.

DID YOU KNOW?
In Jesus' time, Nazareth was just a small village of around 200 people. Today it is the largest city in the north of Israel, home to more than 60,000 inhabitants.

Then Jesus said, "Today, these words have come true. God has sent me to bring you the Good News of his kingdom."

At first everyone listened to him. Jesus spoke well, and they were astonished at the things he was saying to them. Then gradually they began to whisper to each other, "This is the carpenter's son, isn't it? Who does he think he is? How can he say such things?"

"A prophet is never believed by his own people," Jesus said to them.

The crowd became angry then, and they seized Jesus, intending to do him harm. Jesus, however, managed to slip away to safety. He never went back to Nazareth. Instead he went to other towns and villages, telling the Good News about God's kingdom, and healing people who were sick.

Jesus calls the first disciples
Mark 1:16–20

Jesus needed friends to help him with his work. As he walked down by the Sea of Galilee, he saw some fishermen casting their net into the water to catch fish. They were brothers: Simon and Andrew.

Jesus called to them and they came back to the shore.

"Follow me," said Jesus, "and I will make you fishers of people." At once, the two men left their nets to join him, for they knew Jesus was the promised Messiah.

A little further on, Jesus came to the brothers James and John. They were in their father's fishing boat mending the nets with their father, Zebedee.

When Jesus called to them, they immediately left the boat and their father and followed him. They, too, knew that Jesus was sent by God.

Jesus chose these men not because they were clever or gifted, but because he knew they were strong, honest and loyal to God. He would later give Simon a new name: Peter, which means, "rock". And James and John he called the "sons of thunder" because they were keen, fiery young men.

Instead of gathering fish into their nets, Simon Peter, Andrew, James and John would gather people into the kingdom of God.

These four disciples stayed close to Jesus always, learning from him and helping him as he travelled the country, teaching and healing.

DID YOU KNOW?
A disciple is someone who follows and learns from a leader, or master. Jesus called, or chose, twelve disciples to follow him.

The marriage feast at Cana
John 2:1–12

One day, Jesus was invited with his mother, Mary, and his disciples to a wedding at Cana. During the feast, Mary noticed that the wine was running out. Soon there would be nothing for the wedding guests to drink!

Mary told Jesus. "Please do something," she said to him, "or the feast will be spoiled and the bridegroom and his family will be embarrassed."

Jesus reminded his mother that the time to do his heavenly Father's work had not yet arrived, but Mary was sure he would help. She called the stewards over.

"Just do whatever he tells you," she told them.

It was the custom in those days for guests to wash themselves before an important meal, and large jars of water were provided for them to use as they came in the house.

Jesus noticed the row of six large water jars standing against the wall: each could hold about twenty or thirty gallons.

DID YOU KNOW?

The custom at the time was to serve guests the best wine at the start of celebrations, then change to wine of lesser quality after it had been drunk.

"Fill these jars with water," he told the servants. They quickly filled them all to the brim. "Now pour some out and take it to the wine steward to taste," he said.

They did as he said. The wine steward tasted the water and it had turned into delicious wine!

"I see you've left the best wine until last!" he said to the bridegroom. Of course, he had no idea where it had come from.

This was the first miracle Jesus performed, and it showed his disciples that he was indeed from God.

Jesus heals many
Mark 1:29–31

Jesus went down to Capernaum, on the shore of the Sea of Galilee, and began teaching people about the kingdom of God. Capernaum was an important, busy town, with a garrison of Roman soldiers and a tax office. Many traders and travellers would have passed through it, and from here Jesus was able to go out to the other towns and villages of Galilee.

Capernaum was also the home of Simon Peter where he and his wife shared a house with his mother-in-law.

Jesus used to teach in the synagogue, where everyone who heard him was impressed because he spoke with great authority. One Sabbath Jesus healed a man with a troubled mind, and the people were astonished at his power. They began to talk about him and word spread all round the surrounding countryside.

That day, after the service, Simon Peter took Jesus back to his house for dinner. When they arrived, they discovered that Simon Peter's mother-in-law was in bed, very ill with a fever. Jesus stood over her and commanded the fever to leave her. Immediately it went.

That evening there was no peace in Simon Peter's house. The fame of Jesus had spread, and by sunset a crowd of people had gathered outside the house. They were all suffering in some way or another and came for healing. Jesus did not send them away but laid his hands on each of them and cured them.

Early next morning, Jesus left the house to find a quiet place to pray. But the crowds followed him and tried to persuade him to stay with them. "No," he said. "I must proclaim the kingdom of God to others, too, for that is what I was sent to do."

DID YOU KNOW?
Jesus performed many miracles,
including healing the sick and
restoring the dead to life.

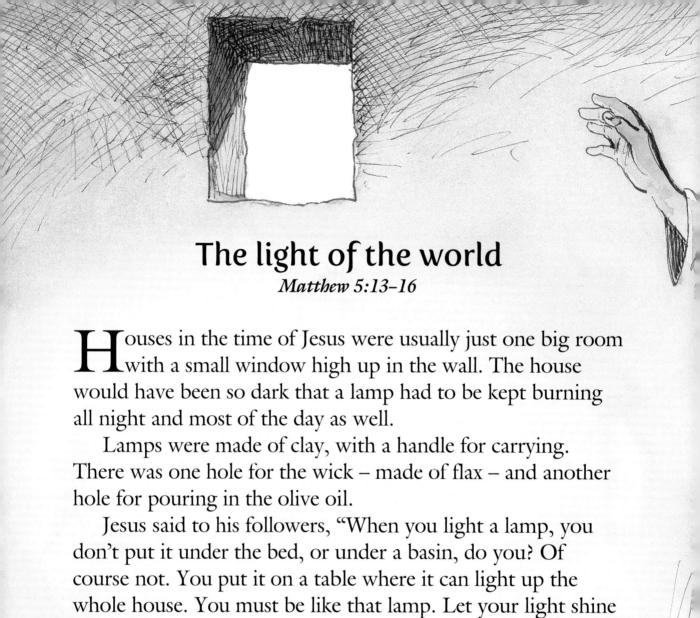

The light of the world
Matthew 5:13–16

Houses in the time of Jesus were usually just one big room with a small window high up in the wall. The house would have been so dark that a lamp had to be kept burning all night and most of the day as well.

Lamps were made of clay, with a handle for carrying. There was one hole for the wick – made of flax – and another hole for pouring in the olive oil.

Jesus said to his followers, "When you light a lamp, you don't put it under the bed, or under a basin, do you? Of course not. You put it on a table where it can light up the whole house. You must be like that lamp. Let your light shine out for everyone so that they can see the love and goodness of God shining in everything you do. Be a good example for them. They will see that your light comes from God and will give him thanks and praise."

DID YOU KNOW?
The candle in a Christingle symbolises Jesus Christ as the light of the world.

Jesus taught his followers all about the kingdom of God, and he was the perfect example of love and obedience to his heavenly Father. The apostle, John, wrote that Jesus was "The light of men, a light that shines in the dark, a light that darkness could not overpower."

And Jesus himself said, "I am the light of the world. Whoever follows me will not be walking in the dark; he will have the light of life."

So when Jesus sent his disciples out to be the Light of the World, they knew exactly what he meant.

Jesus teaches about prayer
Matthew 6:1–15

Jesus often went off by himself to pray. One day, when he returned from one of these sessions, the disciples asked him to teach them how they should pray.

"When you pray," said Jesus, "don't pray in the open, where everyone will see you. Instead, go to your room and shut the door. God sees and hears everything, and he will hear your prayer. Speak directly to God:

Our Father in heaven,
hallowed be your name,
Your kingdom come,
your will be done,
on earth as it is in heaven.
Give us this day our daily bread,
and forgive us our sins,
as we forgive the sins of others.
Lead us not into temptations,
but keep us safe from evil.

Ask, and it will be given
Matthew 7:7–14

Jesus told his followers, "Ask in prayer, and it will be given to you. Search for God, and you will find him. Knock, and he will open the door to you. Those who ask will receive, those who seek will find, and the door is opened for those who knock.

"What caring father would give his son a stone when he asks for bread? Or would give him a snake when he asks for fish? If you who are weak know what is good for your children, how much more will your heavenly Father give good things to those who ask him."

DID YOU KNOW?
The word 'amen' has its roots in the Hebrew word for 'truth'. It means 'so be it'.

Jesus calls a tax collector

Mark 2:13–17

Levi was a tax collector in the town of Capernaum. It was his job to collect taxes for the Romans from the people of the town, as well as the many traders and fishermen that brought goods by sea into the busy port.

Everyone hated the Romans who had conquered Palestine, and they hated even more the men who collected taxes for them. Often the tax collectors charged more than was needed and kept the extra for themselves.

As Jesus went by the customs house he saw Levi sitting at the table, counting his money, and called to him. "Come, Levi. Follow me."

DID YOU KNOW?
Jerusalem became part of the Roman Empire when it was conquered by the Roman general Pompey in 63 BC.

Without a second thought, Levi left everything to follow this man he had heard so much about.

That night, Levi gave a party at his house in honour of Jesus, his new friend. He invited all his other friends – many of them were hated tax collectors like him – so they could meet Jesus, too. When the officials at the temple heard of the party, they complained to Jesus, "Why do you sit at the same table, eating and drinking with such evil men?"

But Jesus told them, "People who are well do not need a doctor. I have not come to help people who already love and serve God. I have come to help those who are in need of God's forgiveness."

The man who was paralysed
Matthew 9:1–8

One day four men came to the house where Jesus was teaching, carrying a friend on a stretcher. The man was paralysed and could not walk, and his friends believed Jesus could heal him. They could not get past the crowds in the house, so they carried their friend up to the flat roof. Removing some of the roof tiles, they then lowered the stretcher down gently until it came to rest on the floor in front of Jesus. Jesus was pleased with their faith in him. He said to the paralysed man, "My friend, your sins are forgiven."

This made some of the people in the crowd very angry. "Only God can forgive sins," they said.

Jesus knew what they were saying. "Which is easier?" he asked them. "To say to this man, 'Your sins are forgiven,' or 'Get up and walk'? To prove to you that I am the Son of God and able to forgive sins, I say to this man, 'Get up, pick up your stretcher and go home!'"

To the shock and amazement of everyone in the room, the man got up from his stretcher, rolled it up and walked away.

They all praised God. "We've never seen anything like this before!" they said.

DID YOU KNOW?
The Gospels recount 35 miracles that Jesus performed. But **John 21:25** tells us that many more went unrecorded.

The centurion's servant
Matthew 8:5–13

At Capernaum there lived a Roman centurion – an army officer. His servant was very ill and dying. The centurion had heard about Jesus, so he asked some of the Jewish elders to go to Jesus and ask him for his help.

As Jesus approached the town, the elders came to him and told him about the centurion. "He is a good man," they said, "and worthy of your help. He built the synagogue for us and has been very kind to our people."

Jesus agreed to go and see him. But before he reached the centurion's house, however, some of the centurion's friends came to meet him with a message.

They told him that the centurion had said: "Sir, do not put

yourself to any trouble for me. Like you I am a person who commands great authority: I only have to say to one of my soldiers, 'Go!' and he goes, or to another, 'Come here!' and he comes." But I am not worthy for you to enter my house, and for this reason I did not come to you myself. Please just say the word and my servant will be healed."

When Jesus heard the centurion's message, he was astonished. He turned to the crowd of people following him and said, "Not in the whole of Israel have I come across faith such as this."

The messengers returned to the centurion's house and found his servant completely healed.

A woman in the crowd
Luke 8:40–48

There was always a crowd of people around Jesus wherever he went. Some wanted to be healed by him, or ask him to heal someone for them.

One day there was a woman in the crowd who had been ill for many years. She had spent all her money paying doctors to cure her, but their treatments had not helped her. In fact, she was getting worse.

She believed in Jesus and his wonderful powers of healing, and was determined to get close to him. "If I can just touch his clothes," she thought, "I know I will be well again." At last

DID YOU KNOW?
Medical knowledge was more advanced in biblical times than you might think. In **Numbers 19:18**, God instructed Moses to use hyssop for purification. Hyssop oil has since been proven to have antifungal and antibacterial properties.

she touched the hem of Jesus' cloak and she knew at once that she had been cured.

Suddenly, Jesus stopped. He knew power had gone out of him. "Who touched my cloak?" he asked.

The disciples were astonished. "With all these people pressing round you, how can you ask that question?"

But Jesus continued to look all round the crowd. Then the woman came forward, fell at his feet trembling with fear, and admitted what she had done.

"My daughter," said Jesus kindly, "your faith has healed you. Go in peace and be free of your illness."

The daughter of Jairus
Mark 5:35–43

One day, Jairus, who was the head of the synagogue – the Jewish place of worship – pushed through the crowd and fell at Jesus' feet, weeping. "Master," he cried, "my only daughter is dying. Please come, I know you can save her."

"I'll come at once," said Jesus. But on the way Jesus and Jairus were met by one of Jairus' servants. "It's too late," he said to Jairus. "Your daughter is dead."

"Don't worry," said Jesus. "Just have faith and she will be safe."

When they finally arrived at the house, Jesus sent away

all the weeping mourners at the house of Jairus.

"The child is not dead," Jesus told them. "She's just asleep." But they only laughed at him.

Jesus went in to the little girl and took her hand. "Come! Get up!" he said to her. The girl opened her eyes. Then she sat up.

"She is hungry," said Jesus to the girl's astonished parents. "You must give her something to eat. But don't tell anyone about what has happened here today."

DID YOU KNOW?
The resurrection of Jairus' daughter was the first recorded miracle of this kind performed by Jesus. He also saved the widow's son at Nain and, perhaps most famously, Lazarus.

The loaves and fishes
Mark 6:30–44

Jesus sent his twelve disciples out into the countryside to continue his work of teaching and healing among the people. When they returned, he could see they were very tired and needed to rest. So they set off by boat, heading for a quiet place near Bethsaida where they could be by themselves.

However, some people saw them leave and guessed where they were going. Before long, people from all the towns and villages around were hurrying to get there ahead of them. When Jesus stepped ashore, he could see a huge crowd waiting for him and he felt sorry for them.

DID YOU KNOW?
The feeding of the five thousand is the only miracle that is mentioned in all four Gospels. This suggests that it was of great importance to the early Christian Church.

"They are like sheep without a shepherd," he said. Jesus talked to them for some time.

As the day drew to a close, the disciples said to Jesus. "It's getting late," they said. "You should send these people to the villages, away from this lonely place, so they can get food."

"Give them something to eat yourselves," said Jesus. They were shocked. "Are we to spend a fortune on bread for them all?"

"How many loaves and fish do you have?" he asked.

They counted that they had five loaves and two fish. Jesus told them to gather the people together in groups. He took the loaves and fish and looked up to heaven and gave thanks. Then he handed them to his disciples and instructed them to share out the food among the people.

There were over five thousand people in the crowd: everyone ate as much as they wanted.

Jesus walks on the water
Matthew 14:22–33

Jesus sent his disciples off in the boat while he sent the crowds away. He promised to join them at Bethsaida, but in the meantime he went off by himself to pray.

By evening, the boat was far out on the Sea of Galilee. There were strong winds blowing, and very soon the disciples were worn out trying to row against them.

Jesus knew that they were in trouble, so he walked across the surface of the sea towards them.

When the disciples saw him approaching, they were terrified. "It is a ghost!" they cried.

"Do not be afraid, said Jesus. "It is I."

Simon Peter then said, "Lord, if it is really you, then tell me to come to you across the water."

DID YOU KNOW?
The phrase "do not be afraid" appears 365 times in the Bible; that's the same number of times as there are days in the year.

"Come!" said Jesus, holding out his hands.

Simon Peter cautiously stepped out of the boat and put his feet on the water. He took a few steps towards Jesus and sure enough he, too, was able to walk on the surface of the sea. It felt marvellous! But suddenly Simon Peter felt the strength of the wind against him, and he became afraid. Then he started to sink.

"Help me, Lord!" he cried. "I'm sinking!"

Jesus put out his hand at once and held him. "Why did you doubt? Do you have such little faith?"

As they both got into the boat, the wind dropped. The others in the boat were stunned at what they had seen.

Peter believes in Jesus
Matthew 16:13–20

Jesus and his disciples crossed over the Sea of Galilee to the coast of Caesarea Philippi, on the other side, away from the crowds. There, Jesus was able to teach them and warn them all to be on their guard against the strict Jews – the Pharisees and Sadducees – who would try and destroy their faith in him. Then he asked "Who do people say that I am?"

"Some say you are John the Baptist," they said. "Others think you are Elijah, or Jeremiah, or one of the other prophets."

"But who do you think I am?" asked Jesus.

Simon Peter spoke out immediately. "You are Christ, the Messiah, son of the living God."

Jesus said to Simon Peter, "You are blessed, because my Father in heaven himself has revealed this truth to you. And so I now tell you that you are Peter – a name that means rock – and it is upon you that I will build my church. It will stand firm and solid against the forces of evil. And you shall be given the keys of heaven, too."

Jesus rebukes Peter
Matthew 16:21–23

Jesus ordered his disciples not to tell anyone that they knew he was the promised Messiah. He told them that he had to go to Jerusalem, where he would suffer and die at the hands of the Jewish leaders. But on the third day he would rise again from death.

The disciples were appalled. Like other faithful Jews at that time, they all thought that the Messiah was going to lead them all in to the glory of God's kingdom. What was all this talk of suffering and death?

Peter took Jesus to one side. "This must not happen to you, Lord!" he cried out.

Jesus turned away. "You are trying to stop me from fulfilling my purpose! Peter, you are thinking only of yourself, not of the things of God and others."

Only by giving his life for us could Jesus become our Saviour.

DID YOU KNOW?
Many times throughout the Bible, Jesus asks people to keep secret his identity as the Son of God.

Jesus is transfigured
Matthew 17:1-13

A week later, Jesus took his closest disciples – Peter, James and John – high up a mountain where they could pray in solitude.

While they were praying, the appearance of Jesus suddenly changed: his face shone like the sun and his clothes became brighter than the snow on the mountain. Two other figures appeared alongside Jesus, talking with him. They were the prophets Moses and Elijah.

Peter, James and John were astonished.

DID YOU KNOW?

The famous Italian Renaissance artist Raphael died shortly before finishing his painting, *The Transfiguration*. It is believed that his pupil, Giulio Romano, completed work on it.

Then a cloud covered Jesus and a voice said, "This is my beloved Son. Listen to him."

The disciples fell to the ground, covering their faces. When they looked up again, they saw only Jesus. He walked down the mountain with them and warned them not to tell anyone what they had seen until after his resurrection. But they were too scared to ask him what he meant.

The parable of the sower
Matthew 13:1–9

Jesus told his followers many parables. One day he asked the crowd gathered around him to imagine a farmer going out to sow seed in his field. The farmer scattered seed by hand as he walked up and down his field. "As the farmer sowed," said Jesus, "some seed fell on the path, and the birds flew down and ate it. Some fell on to rocky ground where there wasn't much soil. It grew quickly, then shrivelled and died in the scorching sun. Some seed fell into thorns, which grew up and choked it. But some seed fell into rich soil and grew tall and strong, producing a good harvest.

"The seed is the Word of God. Some people hear the Word, but the Devil hardens their hearts and they soon forget what they have heard. Some hearts are too shallow, like rocky ground; the Word is heard with joy at first, but it does not last. Others hear the Word but are more interested in worldly things, like becoming rich, and the Word is choked like the seed amongst the thorns. But some people hear the Word and accept it, giving a rich harvest of faith, goodness and love."

DID YOU KNOW?
A parable is a story that helps explain a religious or moral message.

The parable of the good neighbour
Luke 10:25–37

One day, a lawyer asked Jesus to explain the Commandment, 'Love your neighbour as yourself'. "Who is my neighbour?" he asked. Jesus told this story:

A man was travelling from Jerusalem to Jericho, when he was attacked by a gang of robbers. They took his money and clothes, and left him to die. A priest and a Levite – a servant at the temple – both came along the road, but hurried by on the other side without stopping.

Later, a Samaritan traveller came along and when he saw

144

the injured man he went to him. He bandaged the man's wounds and covered him with his own cloak. Then he lifted the man onto his donkey and took him to an inn, where he hired a room and looked after him.

The next day the Samaritan gave two silver coins to the innkeeper. "Take care of this man," he said. "If you spend more than that I'll repay you on my way back."

Jesus asked the lawyer, "Which of these three do you think was a good neighbour to the injured man?"

"The one who was kind to him," the lawyer replied.

"That's right," said Jesus. "Then go and be a good neighbour, just like him."

145

The parable of the lost sheep
Luke 15:1–7

Jesus used stories, known as parables, to explain God's love for everyone. He often compared God to a shepherd looking after us, his flock. One parable Jesus told was this:

There was once a shepherd with a flock of a hundred sheep. Every morning the shepherd led them to places where the grass was good to eat, and every evening led them back down to the safety of the stone fold, when the shepherd counted them to make sure they were all there.

One evening he only counted ninety-nine sheep.

Immediately, the shepherd left his flock in the safety of the sheepfold and went back up the hillside to search for the one sheep that was lost.

For hours he searched. Then, when he found the frightened lamb, he put it across his shoulders and carried it joyfully all the way back to the sheepfold.

When the shepherd finally got home, he was so happy that he called all his family and friends round for a party. "Come and celebrate with me!" he told them. "I have found my lamb that was lost!"

In the same way, Jesus explained, God loves each one of us so much that he rejoices more over one person who comes back to him, than over all the people already safe in his care.

The parable of the lost son
Luke 15:11–24

There was once a rich farmer who had two sons. He loved them both and planned to share out his estate equally between them when he died.

The younger son decided he didn't want to wait that long. So he went to his father and asked him if he could have his share of the money now, while he was still young enough to enjoy it.

The father was sad, but he did as his son asked because he loved him.

The son then went to live in a foreign city, where he had a wonderful time and made many new friends. But before long his money was spent and his friends left him.

In desperation, the son took on a job with a local farmer, feeding his pigs. There were times when he would have gladly eaten the pig food; he was so hungry.

"Here I am dying of hunger," he said to himself, "when even my father's hired servants have more food than they need! I will go back home and say to my father: 'Father, I have behaved badly. I am not fit to be called your son. Please give me a job on your farm!'"

But while he was still a long way off, his father saw him coming and ran to meet him.

The son tried to say the words he had practised, but his father took no notice. Instead he hugged him tightly and called to the servants, "Quick! Bring fine clothes! Prepare a feast! My son was lost – and now he's found!"

DID YOU KNOW?
This parable is sometimes known as the parable of the Prodigal Son. 'Prodigal' is a word used to describe a person who is wasteful or extravagant with money and possessions.

Children and the kingdom

Luke 18:15–17

Jesus showed that God's love was for all people. He was a friend to everyone – especially those who were poor, or sick or unimportant – and particularly children.

One day, the disciples asked Jesus, "Who is the greatest in the kingdom of heaven?"

Jesus knew that they were really asking about how they could become powerful themselves. Before he answered their question, Jesus called over a little boy who was playing in front of them, sat him on his knee and put his arms round him.

"You see this child?" he asked them. "Well, unless your hearts change and you become as obedient and trusting as this little child, you will not be able to enter the kingdom of heaven.

"Anyone who welcomes children in my name, welcomes me," said Jesus. "But make sure you never treat children badly, because their angels in heaven are always close to God, looking after them."

People often brought their children to Jesus, so he could say a prayer over them. His friends tried to send them away, but Jesus said, "Do not stop the children coming to me. It is to children like these that the kingdom of heaven belongs."

DID YOU KNOW?

Psalm 127:3 teaches us that: "Children are a heritage from the Lord, the fruit of the womb a reward from him."

The way to pray
Luke 11:5–13

Jesus said, "When you pray, tell God what you need. Be sure that he will answer your prayer, and don't be afraid to keep on asking.

"Just suppose a friend of yours arrives without warning in the middle of the night. He's tired and hungry, but you have no food in the house. So you go round to a neighbour to ask for help. 'Can you please lend me some bread?' you call. 'My friend's just arrived and I've nothing to give him to eat!'

"Your neighbour is probably going to be annoyed.

152

DID YOU KNOW?

An 'intercessory prayer' is when you pray on behalf of someone else, to benefit them, not yourself. For example, you might pray that a friend recovers from an illness, or that a family member makes a safe return from a journey.

'Go away!' he says, 'it's the middle of the night and my family and I are trying to sleep!' But you don't go away. You keep on asking and knocking until your neighbour finally gives you everything you need, just to make you leave him in peace.

"This is how you should pray," said Jesus. "Don't give up. Ask, and God will give it to you. Look for him, and you will find him. Knock, and he will open the door to you himself, for he never turns anyone away."

Jesus at Bethany
John 12:1–8

The feast of the Passover was drawing near. Jesus and his disciples journeyed to Jerusalem and stopped at the village of Bethany, at the house of some friends, the sisters Martha and Mary, and their brother Lazarus, whom Jesus had earlier restored to life.

That evening they sat down to dinner, which Martha served for them. During the meal, Mary came in with a jar of very expensive perfumed oil. Kneeling at Jesus' feet, she poured the oil over them, wiping it away with her hair. The air was scented with the fragrance of the oil.

"What a waste! That oil should have been sold and the money given to the poor!" said Judas Iscariot, the disciple who looked after their common fund of money. He didn't say this because he cared for the poor, but because he was a thief and often stole from the fund.

"Leave her alone," said Jesus. "She anointed my feet preparing me for burial. There will always be poor people, but I shall not always be with you."

Judas was so angry that he left the house and went straight to the chief priests of the temple to see how he might betray Jesus to them.

DID YOU KNOW?
Passover is a Jewish festival that is also called the Feast of Unleavened Bread. It marks the exodus of the Jews from Egypt after 400 years of slavery.

Jesus enters Jerusalem

John 12:12–50

On the first day of the Passover week Jesus sent two of his disciples ahead of him, to the village of Bethphage. "You will find a young donkey there, tied up with its mother. Untie it and bring it back with you. If you are asked what you are doing, tell them the Master needs it and will send it back soon."

The disciples found everything just as Jesus had said. They brought the donkey back to Jesus and covered it with their coats to make a saddle. It had never been ridden before, but the donkey willingly allowed Jesus to sit on its back.

And so Jesus travelled into the great city of Jerusalem, not riding the war-horse of a king, but on the back of a humble donkey. The promised Messiah was a king of peace, not war.

Crowds of people rushed into the streets to see Jesus and welcome him. They spread their cloaks on the ground in front of him and shouted "Hosannah!" joyfully praising God and singing, "Blessed is he who comes in the name of the Lord!"

But there was a group of religious men in the crowd, called Pharisees. They did not approve of all the noise and excitement at this holy time, or the way Jesus was so popular with everyone. It only made them want to get rid of him all the more.

DID YOU KNOW?
Zechariah prophesied that this event would happen. "See, your king is coming to you … humble and mounted on … the foal of a donkey." **(Zechariah 9:9)**

As he came in sight of the holy city itself, Jesus became very sad and wept. He knew that Jerusalem would not listen to his message of peace, and would one day be destroyed.

Jesus washes the disciples' feet
John 13:1–20

In those days, it was the custom for the host at a meal to have a servant ready to wash the hot and dusty feet of his guests.

While the disciples were seated at the supper table, Jesus stood up, took off his outer garment and wrapped a towel round his waist. Then he poured water into a basin and began to wash the feet of each of his disciples.

When he reached Peter, however, Peter was horrified. "Lord, are you going to wash my feet?" he asked him.

"You don't understand what I am doing now," Jesus told him, "but it will soon become clear."

"Never!" said Peter. "You shall never wash my feet!" Peter was shocked. It was unthinkable that Jesus should perform such a lowly task.

"If you do not let me wash your feet," said Jesus, "you cannot belong to me."

Then Peter understood. "Then, Lord, don't just wash my feet – wash all of me!"

"No, you are already clean," said Jesus. Then he looked around the table. "But not all of you are." He knew one of them had evil in his heart and would soon betray him.

DID YOU KNOW?

Until 1689, each year on Maundy Thursday the King or Queen of England would wash the feet of the poor in Westminster Abbey. This reminded them that they were there to serve their subjects.

"I have given you all an example to follow," he said. "If I, your Lord and Master, have washed your feet like any ordinary servant, then you too should be servants of each other and be prepared to wash each other's feet."

Judas plots to betray Jesus

Matthew 26:14–16

Of all his disciples, Judas Iscariot alone did not approve of some of the things Jesus did. Judas looked after their common fund, which was used to pay for their simple needs and help the poor, and he was known to have helped himself on occasion. It was easy for Satan to enter his heart.

Judas had secretly gone to see the members of the Jewish council, the Sanhedrin. He knew they wanted to arrest Jesus, and they discussed how he might help.

Judas agreed to their offer of thirty pieces of silver, and the deal was struck.

The last supper
John 13:21–38

It was the feast of Passover, and Jesus knew he would soon die and return to his Father in heaven. During their last supper together, Jesus announced to the disciples that one of them would betray him. John, sitting beside Jesus, leaned over and asked him quietly, "Who is it, Lord?"

"The one to whom I shall give this piece of bread," said Jesus. He handed it to Judas, saying, "Do what you have to do quickly!" The other disciples thought Jesus was telling Judas to give some of their funds to the poor.

As soon as Judas had taken the bread, he slipped away into the night.

After supper Jesus took his disciples out of the city. As they walked he told them, "You will all lose faith tonight and desert me."

Peter protested, saying, "Even if everyone else loses faith, I won't!"

But Jesus answered him, "The rooster will not crow until you have betrayed me three times."

The garden of Gethsemane
Mark 14:32–50

Jesus and his disciples came to a quiet garden of olive trees, called Gethsemane.

There he asked his disciples to wait for him while he took his three closest friends, Peter, James and John, to a lonely part of the garden to pray. He became very troubled and deeply distressed. "My soul is full of sorrow," he told them. "Wait here for me and stay awake."

Jesus went further into the garden and threw himself on the ground, "Father," he prayed, "everything is possible for you. Take this suffering away from me. But let it be as your will, not mine, would be done."

DID YOU KNOW?
The phrase 'kiss of death' is thought to have originated from this famous event.

His friends were so tired; they could not keep their eyes open. Twice Jesus returned to them to find them asleep. The third time he said, "It is all over. Come, get up. My betrayer is here."

Just then Judas Iscariot came up to him, followed by a band of men armed with clubs and swords sent by the chief priests. He greeted Jesus with a kiss: this was the signal for the armed men to seize Jesus.

Terrified, the disciples all ran away.

Judas is sorry
Matthew 27:1–10

Early next morning, the chief priests and elders of the people decided that Jesus should be put to death.

We will never really know why Judas betrayed Jesus. Whatever his reasons, it is clear that Judas had not intended that Jesus should be condemned to death. As soon as he heard that Jesus was to die, Judas was filled with remorse.

He went straight to the Sanhedrin with the thirty pieces of silver he had been given.

"I have made a terrible mistake," Judas said. "I have betrayed an innocent man."

"Why should we worry?" said the chief priests. "That's your problem, not ours."

Appalled, Judas threw the money down in the sanctuary of the temple, and ran out. Unable to bear what he had done, Judas killed himself.

The chief priests picked up the coins from the temple floor and wondered what they should do with them.

"It's blood-money," they said. "Therefore it is against the law for it to be put into the temple treasury."

So they decided to use the money to buy a potter's field, to turn it into a graveyard for foreigners. And even to this day, Jerusalem's cemetery for foreigners is known as the Field of Blood.

DID YOU KNOW?
According to **Exodus 21:32**, the value of a slave's life was 30 pieces of silver.

Peter's denial
John 18:15–27

Peter had been horrified at the things that had happened in the Garden of Gethsemane. He had tried to save Jesus from his attackers, drawing his sword and slashing off the ear of a man called Malchus, the high priest's servant. But then Jesus had commanded him to put his sword away and heal the injured man.

Helpless, Peter could only stand in the shadows and watch while the men bound the master he loved and led him away. He and John followed at a distance, and saw them take Jesus into the palace of Annas, the high priest.

Now John was acquainted with the high priest, so leaving Peter outside, he went in and spoke to the woman on duty at the door, asking her if they could both come inside. As soon as the maid saw Peter she said, "Aren't you another of that man's disciples?"

"No, I'm not!" said Peter, quickly. He went over to the fireside, where the servants and guards were warming themselves.

"You were with him, weren't you?" asked a guard.

"No, my friend," said Peter. "You are mistaken."

Then a servant – a relative of Malchus, in fact – said, "Didn't I see you in the garden with him?"

"No, it wasn't me! I don't know what you are talking about!" shouted Peter.

Just then a cock crowed and Peter remembered Jesus' words: "Before the cock crows you will deny me three times."

He had promised Jesus, "Even if I have to die, I will never deny you!"

Peter ran outside, threw himself on the ground and wept bitterly.

DID YOU KNOW?
Roosters, or cockerels, are sometimes seen as a symbol of watchfulness, because they awake early each day and see dawn's light triumph over the darkness of night.

Jesus before Pilate
Luke 23:1–16

Pilate summoned the chief priests. "You have brought this man, Jesus, before me, accused of crimes against the state," he told them. "Well, I have found no case against him. Neither has Herod: he has sent him back to us. This man has done nothing to deserve death, so I shall have him flogged and then released."

The Jewish leaders were furious. "We want him crucified!" they shouted.

Pilate did not want to cause a riot, but he couldn't just hand over an innocent man to be executed. So he ordered Jesus to be brought before him for questioning again. "Are you really the king of the Jews?" he asked him.

"Is this your own question," said Jesus, "or are you just repeating what others have said?"

"Am I a Jew?" snapped Pilate. "It's your own people and the chief priests who have handed you over to me. What have you done?"

"My kingdom is not of this world," replied Jesus. "If it was, my followers would have fought to save me from my enemies."

"You are a king, then?" said Pilate.

"Yes, I am a king. I was born to bring truth into the world. All those on the side of truth listen to my voice."

"What is truth?" sighed Pilate, heavily as he left Jesus and went back out to face the crowds.

Barabbas the robber
Matthew 27:15–26

It was the custom at the Passover festival for the governor to release a prisoner for the people – anyone they chose. There was a man in prison at that time called Barabbas, who had caused a riot and committed murder. So, when the people came to ask Pilate for the release of a prisoner, Pilate asked them, "Do you want me to release the king of the Jews?" He knew very well that the chief priests were jealous of Jesus and that was why they wanted to get rid of him.

At that moment, Pilate received a message from his wife. She warned her husband not to have anything to do with the death of Jesus of Nazareth. "He is innocent. I have been upset all day by a dream I had about him," she said.

"No," replied the people. "We want Barabbas." The chief priests had already told them what to say.

"What shall I do with the man you call the king of the Jews?" Pilate asked them.

"Crucify him! Crucify him!"

"But what harm has he done?" Pilate pleaded of the crowd. But the people ignored him shouting, "We want Barabbas!"

So Pilate sent for a bowl of water, and in front of the crowds he washed his hands. "I am innocent of this man's blood," he told them.

"His blood be on us and on our children!" shouted the people as Jesus was delivered for crucifixion.

The Crucifixion
John 19:16–37

Jesus was taken outside the city of Jerusalem to a place called Golgotha. He was so weak that the soldiers had to force a man called Simon of Cyrene to carry his great cross. Once there, Jesus was nailed to the cross and raised above the ground. Two thieves were crucified with Jesus, one on either side of him. Jesus prayed: "Father, forgive them. They do not know what they do."

On Pilate's orders a sign was fixed on the cross that read: *Jesus of Nazareth, King of the Jews.* The chief priests told Pilate to change this to read: *This man claimed to be the King of the Jews.* But Pilate replied, "What I have written, I have written."

Standing by the cross with Jesus were his mother Mary, John and Mary Magdalene. Jesus said to his mother, "John is your son, now." And so, John took Mary into his home and looked after her.

The Jewish leaders wanted the bodies of Jesus and the two thieves to be removed before sunset, when the Sabbath began. The soldiers broke the legs of the thieves, but for Jesus, who was already dead, one soldier pierced his side with a lance instead, and immediately blood and water ran down.

Everything happened just as scripture had said it would. Darkness covered the land.

DID YOU KNOW?
It is believed that Jesus died at 3 o'clock in the afternoon. Many churches hold services on Good Friday at this time as a sign of remembrance.

Mary in the garden

John 20:1–18

Joseph of Arimathea, a secret disciple of Jesus, asked Pilate for permission to bury the body of Jesus before the Sabbath day began at sunset. Joseph was helped by his friend, Nicodemus. They wrapped the body and laid it in a new tomb cut out of rock. Then they rolled a huge stone in front of the entrance and went home.

As soon as the Sabbath was over, Mary Magdalene came to the tomb. To her astonishment, she saw the stone had been rolled back from the entrance. The tomb was empty. The woman ran to tell the disciples what she had found, and Peter and one of the others came to see for themselves.

DID YOU KNOW?

Mary Magdalene features prominently in writings that were found sealed inside a ceramic jar discovered in southern Egypt in 1945.

Afterwards, Mary stayed in the garden, weeping.

Someone spoke to her in a gentle voice, asking, "Woman, why are you crying?"

"They have taken my Lord," she sobbed. She thought she was talking to one of the gardeners. "Sir, if you have taken him away, tell me where he is so I can give him a proper burial."

"Mary!" said the stranger, softly.

Mary knew that voice. "Master!" she cried, joyfully, and she threw herself at Jesus.

"Do not cling to me," he said to her, "but go and tell my friends that you have seen me."

The road to Emmaus
Luke 24:13–35

That same day, two disciples were on their way home from Jerusalem to a village called Emmaus. As they walked, talking over the terrible things that had happened in the last few days, Jesus himself came up and walked beside them. But something prevented the two men from recognising him.

"What are you discussing that makes you so sad?" Jesus asked them.

"Haven't you heard?" they replied. "Jesus of Nazareth, the one we believed was the promised Messiah, has been put to death."

Jesus shook his head. "Why are you so slow to believe everything the prophets told you would happen? Didn't they say that the Messiah should suffer and then be glorified?" And beginning with Moses and the prophets he explained to them all the passages in scripture that referred to himself.

When they reached Emmaus, the two disciples invited Jesus to have supper with them. When they sat down to eat, Jesus took up the bread, blessed it and gave it to them. And at that moment, the disciples recognised him. Jesus, however, disappeared.

Immediately the two friends returned to Jerusalem to tell the other disciples their wonderful news.

Jesus appears for the third time
John 21:1–18

Peter, James and John and four other disciples went out fishing one night, but they returned to the shore empty-handed.

A man was waiting for them on the shore. He called out as they brought in the boat: "Have you caught anything?"

"No," they shouted back.

"Throw out the net to starboard and you'll catch some fish," said the stranger.

So they dropped the net into the water again and immediately it became so full of fish that they could not pull it back in.

"It is the Lord!" said John. Peter looked across at the man on the shore, and then he grabbed his cloak and leaped into the water to join Jesus, leaving the others to bring in the catch.

When the others came ashore, Jesus had breakfast ready for them: bread and some fish cooking on a charcoal fire. After they had eaten, Jesus turned to Peter.

"Simon Peter," he said, "do you love me more than these others do?"

Peter answered, "Lord, you know I do."

"Feed my lambs," said Jesus. Then he asked Peter again, "Simon Peter, do you love me?"

Peter said, "Yes, Lord, you know I love you."

Then Jesus asked a third time, "Do you love me?"

Peter was upset that Jesus asked him three times. "Lord, you know everything; you know I love you!"

Jesus said to him, "Feed my sheep."

Then Peter understood, and the shame of his earlier denial of Jesus was lifted from him.

DID YOU KNOW?

The number three is important in Christianity because it relates to the Holy Trinity: the Father, Son and the Holy Spirit. Three is also the number of days that passed before Jesus rose from the dead.

In the upper room
John 20:19–29

Later that day, the disciples met together in the room where they had eaten their last supper with Jesus. The door was locked, because they were afraid of what might happen to them if the Jewish leaders found them.

Suddenly, Jesus was there with them.

"Peace be with you," he said. "Why are you so afraid? See my hands and feet. It's really me!" The disciples were speechless with joy.

Jesus told them he was going to send them out to do his work, just as the Father had sent him. They were to stay hidden until he could send the Holy Spirit to them.

One of the disciples, Thomas, had not been in the room

DID YOU KNOW?
The nickname 'Doubting Thomas' comes from this story. It is still used today to describe those who disbelieve.

at the time. When the others told him Jesus had actually appeared to them, he did not believe them.

"I won't believe until I have seen and touched him for myself," he said.

A few days later, Jesus came again to the room where the disciples were staying. The door was still locked. This time Thomas was with them.

"Peace be with you!" said Jesus, and he turned to Thomas. "See my hands, Thomas. Here, touch my side and believe in me."

Thomas fell to his knees. "My Lord and my God!" he cried.

"You believe because you can see me," said Jesus. "Happy and blessed are those who cannot see me yet believe in me."

The Ascension
Luke 24:50–53

Jesus appeared to his disciples for the last time on the Mount of Olives. "Go and tell the whole world the Good News," he told them. "I shall be with you always, to the end of time." Then he was lifted up and a cloud carried him out of sight, into heaven.

Matthias is chosen
Acts 1:12–26

The disciples went back to Jerusalem to await the Holy Spirit. They were Peter, John, James, Andrew, Philip, Thomas, Bartholomew and Matthew, Simon the Zealot, James (the son of Alphaeus) and Jude. It was dangerous for them to be seen in the city, as the Jews were arresting anyone they suspected of being a follower of Jesus.

One day, Peter stood up and spoke to them all. Jesus had chosen him to care for his church, and from once having been a fearful, simple fisherman, Peter now showed himself to be a strong leader. Their first task, he told the others, was to appoint a disciple to take the place of the traitor, Judas Iscariot. They needed to choose someone who had been with them right from the time when John the Baptist had preached in the desert.

Two candidates were put forward: Joseph Barsabbas and Matthias. The disciples prayed, opening their hearts to God to guide their choice. Then they drew lots and it was Matthias who was to become the twelfth disciple.

DID YOU KNOW?

The number 12 was important to the Jews because it signified perfection. Judas was replaced so that the number of disciples would be made 'perfect' once again.

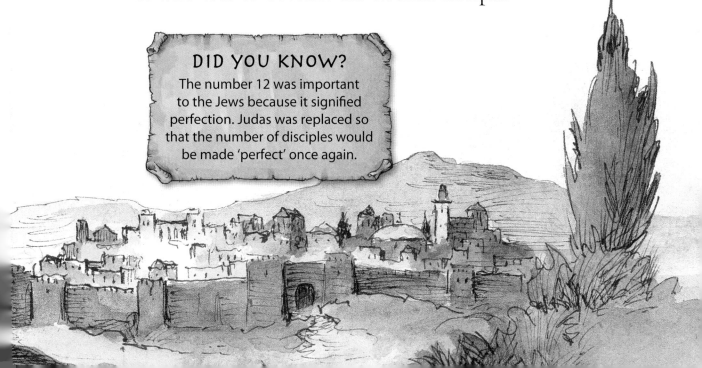

The coming of the Holy Spirit

Acts 2:1–4

Not long after Passover was the Jewish festival of Pentecost. The disciples were praying together in the upper room, when the sound of a rushing wind filled the house. Then flames appeared, which separated and came to rest on the head of each disciple.

They were filled with the Holy Spirit and immediately began to speak in foreign languages.

The Holy Spirit gave them the gift of speech and courage to praise God and proclaim the Good News of Jesus Christ the Saviour.

DID YOU KNOW?
Pentecost is a Greek word meaning 'fiftieth'. The Pentecost Feast, or Feast of Weeks, is so called because it was held 50 days after Passover.

Peter proclaims the Good News

Acts 2:5–41

Devout men from every nation under heaven had gathered in Jerusalem. Yet when the disciples began to preach, they were astounded to be able to understand what they were saying.

Peter addressed the crowd in a loud voice: "Jesus of Nazareth was sent by God, as his miracles proved. You killed him, but God raised him up, freeing him from death. Now the promised Saviour has ascended to God's right hand, in heaven!"

"What should we do?" the crowds asked.

"You must be baptised in the name of Jesus. Then you, too, will receive the gift of the Holy Spirit. This is God's promise to you and your children!"

That day three thousand came to believe in the Good News and were baptised.

The stoning of Stephen

Acts 7:54–60

As the early church grew, the disciples needed help with day-to-day matters such as sharing out food and looking after the poor. Seven men were chosen for this work, one of them a young man called Stephen, who was already filled with the Holy Spirit. He began to work many miracles, so that people came from far and wide to see him.

One day, several Jewish priests came to listen to Stephen and debate the law with him. They wanted to catch him out, but the Holy Spirit always gave Stephen answers to their questions. So they took Stephen to the Sanhedrin, accused of declaring the Jewish law old-fashioned.

DID YOU KNOW?

A martyr is someone who would rather die than give up their religious beliefs. Stephen was the first martyr in the Bible, and was made a saint because of his devotion.

The council members looked at Stephen and it seemed to them that his face shone like that of an angel. "Is it true what these priests have said?" the high priest asked him.

"People have always misunderstood the prophets sent by God," Stephen told them. "You have tried to confine God to a building made by human hands, and resisted the Holy Spirit." The angry council members had Stephen stoned to death.

As he was dying, Stephen prayed: "Lord, receive my spirit. Do not hold this sin against them."

One of the crowd watching was a young man called Saul. Determined to destroy the church, Saul went from house to house arresting anyone who was thought to be a follower of Jesus.

Saul on the road to Damascus
Acts 9:1–22

Saul came from a very religious Jewish family. Such was his zeal for the old Jewish law that he tirelessly hunted down and persecuted all the followers of Jesus. He even asked the high priest in Jerusalem to give him permission to extend his hunt to Damascus, and to bring prisoners back to Jerusalem.

Before he reached the city of Damascus, however, something happened to change his life forever.

A great light from heaven suddenly shone all around Saul, so that he fell to the ground, terrified. Then a voice said, "It is I, Jesus, why do you punish me so?" said the voice. "Get up now and go into the city, and you will be told what you have to do."

The men with Saul were astonished. They had seen the bright light, but not heard the voice. When Saul stood up, he could not see a thing. His friends had to lead him into the city and for three days Saul lay blind, praying and waiting to hear what was to become of him.

DID YOU KNOW?
We say that someone has 'seen the light' when they suddenly become aware of some fact or meaning, just like Saul.

In the city of Damascus there lived a disciple called Ananias. The Lord spoke to him and told him to help Saul. Ananias was horrified. "Lord, I have heard all the harm he has been doing to your faithful people."

But the Lord said, "Go and see him anyway. I have chosen this man to bring my name before people of all nations."

So Ananias went to Saul, saying, "Brother Saul, the Lord Jesus has sent me to heal your sight that you be filled with the Holy Spirit." At once Saul was able to see again and Ananias baptised him. And taking the Roman form of his name, Paul, he began preaching the Good News of Jesus.

Paul and Silas in prison

Acts 16:16–40

Paul and his friends continued to spread the Good News, until one day in Philippi he healed a slave girl of madness. The girl's masters were furious, for they had made a great deal of money out of her ravings, using her to tell fortunes. They seized Paul and Silas and dragged them along to the law court held in the market place, accusing them of breaking the law.

The magistrates found the disciples guilty as charged and ordered them to be flogged and thrown into prison. Their jailer was told to keep a close eye on them, so he chained them to the wall of his most secure cell and fastened their feet in stocks.

Late into the night, the other prisoners could hear Paul and Silas singing and praising God. Suddenly a wild earth tremor shook the prison right down to its foundations. All the doors flew open and the chains fell from all the prisoners.

When the jailer woke and saw the prison doors flung wide, he was terrified that his prisoners had escaped. He drew his sword, intending to kill himself.

"Don't!" shouted Paul. "We are all here!"

The jailer called for lights, and when he saw Paul and Silas he threw himself at their feet. "Sirs, what must I do to be saved?" he asked.

"Believe in the Lord Jesus," they told him, and explained the Good News of Jesus.

That night the jailer and his household were all baptised. Paul and Silas went to the jailer's house for a meal and the whole family celebrated with them.

In the morning, the magistrates sent an order to the jail that Paul and Silas should be released.

DID YOU KNOW?
Earthquakes and tremors are mentioned several times throughout the Bible and were often considered to be God's judgement on actions and events on the earth.

DID YOU KNOW?
Paul's Roman citizenship
saved him many times;
it was against the law for a
Roman citizen to be beaten.

Paul in Jerusalem

Acts 21:17–36

When Paul arrived in Jerusalem the disciples were delighted to see him and hear his news, but they warned him that he had many enemies among the strict Jews in the city, who were accusing Paul of disregarding the Law of Moses.

Paul went to the temple the very next day to show he was still a loyal Jew, but his enemies recognised him. "This is the man who has spoken against the law!" they cried, and suddenly there was uproar as crowds of people surged into the temple and dragged Paul outside.

News of the disturbance reached the commander of the Roman garrison, and he immediately sent out a company of soldiers to break up the mob. Paul was arrested and bound with chains. The only way through the crowd was for the soldiers to carry Paul to safety.

The next day, the commander summoned the Jewish council to find out exactly what charge they wanted brought against Paul.

DID YOU KNOW?
Like the Greeks, the Romans worshipped many gods, as well as worshipping their leader, or Caesar.

Paul a prisoner in Caesarea

Acts 24:22–25:12

Felix, the Roman governor at Caesarea, kept Paul a prisoner for two years. During that time Paul was free to be visited by his friends and receive anything he needed. Felix sent for Paul frequently, pretending to be interested in what Paul had to say, but really he hoped Paul would pay him money for his freedom.

After this, a new governor was appointed: a man called Festus. He was anxious to keep the peace with the Jews, so he continued to keep Paul a prisoner and summoned the chief priests from Jerusalem to state their case against Paul. They made many serious charges against Paul, but they did not have any evidence to prove the truth in the charges.

"I have not committed any offence against Jewish law, or the temple, or Caesar!" said Paul, in his defence.

"Would you be willing to go back to Jerusalem to face these charges before me there?" asked the governor.

Now Paul was a Roman citizen – a status that gave him a number of privileges. It was his right to bring his case before the Emperor, Caesar himself, if he chose to.

"If I have in fact committed any serious crime," he replied to Festus, "I would certainly accept even the death penalty. But I have done nothing wrong. Therefore I appeal to Caesar."

Festus discussed Paul's answer with his advisors, and seeing he had no other option said, "Very well. You have appealed to Caesar; to Caesar you shall go!"

Paul comes to Rome

Acts 28:16–31

News of Paul's coming had already reached the Christian brotherhood in Rome, and some of the brothers came out to meet him. After his tiring journey, their warm welcome put new heart into Paul and he thanked God for them.

And so at long last Julius delivered Paul safely into Rome. It would take some time before his appeal to the Emperor could be arranged, and in the meantime he was allowed to stay in his own private lodgings, which he paid for himself. But a Roman soldier guarded him at all times.

Paul remained under house arrest for two years. During that time he was always busy and kept in touch with the other churches he had helped set up, receiving visitors from far and wide, and continuing to teach the truth about Jesus.

In particular, he was able to write or dictate long letters to various churches and brothers in Christ, and some of these have survived to form part of the New Testament.

Faithful to the end
Timothy 4:1–18

One of the last letters that Paul wrote was to Timothy, who became one of the leaders of the early church and whom, Paul loved as a son.

Paul gave a great deal of advice and encouragement to Timothy, for he knew that his own life was drawing to a close, and he was anxious that Timothy should not grow discouraged during the difficult times ahead. There were people in Rome working against Paul, and when he attended his first defence hearing, all the witnesses who had promised to give evidence for him failed to turn up.

"Be careful always to choose the right course," wrote Paul. "Be brave under trial. Make the proclaiming of the Good News your life's work."

"As for me," he continued, "my life is already being poured away as an offering, and the time has come for me to be gone. I have fought the good fight to the end; I have run the race to the finish; I have kept the faith. All there is to come now is the crown of righteousness reserved for me, which the Lord, the righteous judge, will give me on that Day – and not only to me, but to all those who have longed for him.

"The Lord will rescue me from all evil and bring me safely to his heavenly kingdom. To him be glory forever and ever. Amen."

The Holy Land

Bethsaida

Capernaum

Sea of Galilee

GALILEE

Mt Carmel

Cana

Nazareth

Great Sea (Mediterranean Sea)

Megiddo

Jezreel

GILEAD

Caesarea

SAMARIA

Samaria

River Jordan

ISRAEL

Arimathea

Bethel

Joppa

Emmaus

Jericho

JERUSALEM ■

Bethany

JUDEA

Bethlehem

PHILISTIA

Dead Sea

Gaza

Hebron

JORDAN

Beersheba

◀ *EGYPT*